CAMBRIDGE LIBRARY COLLECTION

Books of enduring scholarly value

Spiritualism and Esoteric Knowledge

Magic, superstition, the occult sciences and esoteric knowledge appear regularly in the history of ideas alongside more established academic disciplines such as philosophy, natural history and theology. Particularly fascinating are periods of rapid scientific advances such as the Renaissance or the nineteenth century which also see a burgeoning of interest in the paranormal among the educated elite. This series provides primary texts and secondary sources for social historians and cultural anthropologists working in these areas, and all who wish for a wider understanding of the diverse intellectual and spiritual movements that formed a backdrop to the academic and political achievements of their day. It ranges from works on Babylonian and Jewish magic in the ancient world, through studies of sixteenth-century topics such as Cornelius Agrippa and the rapid spread of Rosicrucianism, to nineteenth-century publications by Sir Walter Scott and Sir Arthur Conan Doyle. Subjects include astrology, mesmerism, spiritualism, theosophy, clairvoyance, and ghost-seeing, as described both by their adherents and by sceptics.

Mesmeric Experiences

Spencer Timothy Hall (1812–1885) was a writer and practitioner of mesmerism. He grew up in rural Nottinghamshire, apprenticed himself to a printer, and in 1836 he started his own printing business. He later became co-editor of the Sheffield newspaper *The Iris,* and published several books describing the countryside. After watching a demonstration of mesmerism in 1841 Hall became a practitioner himself, demonstrating mesmerism throughout Britain and offering treatment. His most famous patient was Harriet Martineau, who became an enthusiastic supporter of the technique. This book, first published in 1845, describes Hall's first encounter with mesmerism and explains his decision to become a mesmerist. He discusses thirty-four cases in which mesmerism apparently cured medical problems and describes the treatment he gave to Harriet Martineau. This fascinating book provides valuable insights into both the practice and theory of mesmerism in the early Victorian period.

Mesmeric Experiences

SPENCER TIMOTHY HALL

CAMBRIDGE
UNIVERSITY PRESS

CAMBRIDGE UNIVERSITY PRESS

Cambridge, New York, Melbourne, Madrid, Cape Town, Singapore,
São Paolo, Delhi, Dubai, Tokyo, Mexico City

Published in the United States of America by Cambridge University Press, New York

www.cambridge.org
Information on this title: www.cambridge.org/9781108027410

© in this compilation Cambridge University Press 2011

This edition first published 1845
This digitally printed version 2011

ISBN 978-1-108-02741-0 Paperback

MESMERIC

EXPERIENCES.

BY

SPENCER T. HALL,

AUTHOR OF

" THE FORESTER'S OFFERING," " RAMBLES IN THE COUNTRY," ETC.,
AND EDITOR OF THE " PHRENO-MAGNET."

LONDON:

H. BAILLIERE, 219, REGENT STREET,
AND J. OLLIVIER, 59, PALL MALL ;

MACLACHLAN AND STEWART, EDINBURGH; WILLIAM LANG, GLASGOW ;
AND ALL BOOKSELLERS.

1845.

[ENTERED AT STATIONERS' HALL.]

C. WHITING, BEAUFORT HOUSE, STRAND.

TO THE FRIENDS

WHO HAVE STOOD TRUE TO HIM IN THE HOUR OF TRIAL,

THIS LITTLE WORK IS INSCRIBED,

WITH THE UNDIMINISHED ESTEEM AND

GRATITUDE OF

THE AUTHOR.

PREFACE.

————

MAGNETISM and MESMERISM are analogous in their derivation, and, as scientific terms, are alike purely conventional. The first, according to tradition, is from Magnes, a shepherd of Mount Ida, who, discovering the adhesion of loadstone to the metallic end of his crook, made the fact known to mankind, and gave his name to the principle. Mesmer, a modern German physician, having observed the manifestation of a similar principle in the affinity of animal bodies, and shown how one may through this agency be imbued with the qualities of another, has in like manner transmitted his own name with his theory—the practice independent of theory having been common in all ages. The Author's reason for adopting the term Mesmerism in preference to that of Magnetism, is merely that it has, from the circumstances named, a more specific signification, and is, from its frequent use by writers on the subject, become more popular. If, however, an

equally convenient and *still more significant* name could
be given, he would be one of the first to adopt it; but
hitherto, though several other terms have been suggested
to him, none of them seemed to possess both those desi-
derata. Valentine Greatrakes, who cured diseases by
passes and stroking a hundred years before the time
of Mesmer, was endowed with dignity, modesty, and
benignity so evident, that were it not for its want of
euphony the Author would have adopted his name
rather than that of Mesmer, because of his priority and
the beauty of his character. But as it is more with
the use than the worship of a name we are now concerned, the candid Reader will not quarrel with words
provided he be able clearly to comprehend their meaning. This it is hoped, will be a sufficient apology for
those employed in the narrative here submitted to his
perusal and verdict.

> 59, Pall Mall, London,
> Sept. 11, 1845.

ERRATA.

Page 3, line 16, for Chaburns, read Chadburns.
Page 10, line 24, for "hypotism," read "hypnotism.'
Page 27, line 27, for *soubriquet,* read *sobriquet.*

CONTENTS.

CHAPTER I.

CHAPTER VII.

CHAPTER VIII.

CHAPTER IX.

CHAPTER X.

MESMERIC EXPERIENCES.

CHAPTER I.

IT was by invitation, as a member of the press, that
I first attended a mesmeric conversazione. The lamp-
lit room in which it was held was large and lofty, and
the company numerous. An ample platform was ele-
vated at the end and was occupied on my entrance by
the experimenter, whose appearance was calculated to
awaken curiosity and wonder in a high degree. He
was about middle age, slightly above middle size, with
a well-set muscular frame, and was clothed in black.
His hair was dark, his eye bold, powerful, and steady;
and his beard, which was very profuse, descended to his
breast. This was M. La Fontaine, who, as the prelimi-
naries to the evening's operations proceeded, was joined
by one and then others, to the number of half-a-dozen
medical men and lawyers, all characterised by an air of
mixed importance, anxiety, and acuteness, as though
upon them devolved the duty of there, then, and for
ever laying open a profound mystery, or exploding a
cheat. The audience at first was evidently under the

B

influence of uncertainty as to whether the experimenter, who spoke only in French, should be most regarded as a deluded mystic or a designing quack. To suppose him at once a rational and honest man seemed out of the question. This feeling was, however, considerably changed before the close of the experiments, which were somewhat as follows:—

A young and slender woman, of a dull rather than an excitable temperament, and dressed in black, slowly ascended the platform, and was placed in a chair. Two of the medical men having reported the state of her pulse, the mysterious-looking mesmerist now approached, and deliberately taking her hands, placed his thumbs to hers; their eyes met, for about five minutes there was an intense mutual gaze; and then, as the lids began to quiver, the pupils turned up, her respiration faltered, her head slowly fell, and breathing out a protracted sigh, she passed, or appeared to pass, into a deep and stolid sleep. Slow passes were now made from her head to her feet, her arms were gently raised and made rigid by the manipulations of the operator, and thus they remained nearly the space of two hours horizontally extended, without quivering or flinching; whilst snuff, ammonia, lighted matches, and even a burning candle, were repeatedly applied to her lips and nose, and pins and lancets to her fingers, cheeks, and eyelids. The following night I attended again. The same inductive process was repeated with some trifling variations, followed by the same barbarities in the name of tests, with the additional one of a galvanic battery made to bear upon the patient with a force six times greater than could have been sustained by any medical man in the company, but without producing any further effect upon her than there would have been upon a corpse! Some of the audience applauded, whilst others deprecated these proceedings. No rational being could doubt the abnormal condition of the woman, whatever might be the medium through which it had been induced, and I departed from the scene with mingled feelings of curiosity and awe, still dubious as to the extent to which this power might be commanded by the generality of men, and whether those susceptible to it were few or many.

In a very short time I became more enlightened on these matters. Among those who had taken part with M. La Fontaine in these experiments, and watched with no ordinary acuteness their bearing at every point, was our distinguished townsman, Dr. G. Calvert Holland, who endeavoured, as a more rational test than any of those he had seen tried, to produce similar effects upon some of his own family and domestics, in which he soon succeeded even to a greater degree. I forgot to say that these occurrences were at Sheffield, where several other highly intelligent residents, including the Chaburns, opticians, Mr. John Fowler, and Mr. John Rodgers, soon brought further evidence before inquirers, and mesmerising became general throughout the neighbourhood. It is to associating with the last-named gentlemen that I owe much of my initiatory knowledge. We very frequently experimented together, and freely opened our views on what transpired to each other.

A private society, composed of the leading scientific men of the town, was also established for the investigation of mesmeric phenomena, and of this I was elected an honorary member in consequence of some apparently new and interesting experiments to which I had incidentally drawn attention; but then, and for some time after, there was no likelihood of my becoming so publicly identified with the question as events have made me. From childhood I had been a student of Nature in her various phases, and had watched her unfoldings everywhere with a loving eye and heart. Having communed with her in the silence and solitude of the mountain-top, and where old forests whispered their deep music to the inner sense; having also in an open and passive mood allowed human life and action, as it were by a species of mental photography, to make their legitimate impress upon my soul, I now determined to receive in the same spirit whatever might be revealed to me through the agency of mesmerism—to be unresisting as a child, with Truth for my teacher; and having avoided all importuning on the one hand, and thwarting on the other, to be thankful for whatever information might be thus obtained. It is simply the reflex of what was so learned I am giving to the world in the following pages.

CHAPTER II.

THE AUTHOR TRIES EXPERIMENTS—CHARACTER OF THE PHENO-
MENA—SUPPOSED ILLUSTRATIONS OF PHRENOLOGY.

THE beginning of my career as a mesmeric experimenter, was as purely incidental and simple as that of
my acquaintance with the experiments of others. Being
deeply interested in phrenology, and enjoying some
reputation among my friends as a manipulator, I was
one evening selected by a party to try experiments for
testing the (then) newly-propounded theory of Phreno-
mesmerism. Our patient was a young man of the
name of Joseph Flower, who had first been rendered
somnolent by Mr. Rodgers making passes over the top
of his head and along the course of the spine, whilst
standing behind him. As he became more susceptible,
he could be rendered rigid or flexible, or be attracted
and repelled, by the operator at a considerable distance,
the intervention of a stone wall, or any other solid and
opaque body, presenting no obstacle to the influence;
and it is a well-attested fact, that on one occasion he
was most powerfully affected when the operator was
distant not less than three miles. Such, however, were
the results of that experiment as to forbid any repetition of it.*

On the evening in question, Flower having been
thrown into a profound mesmeric sleep by Mr. Rodgers,
we were placed *en rapport,* and on being gently pressed

* See Mr. J. Fowler's letter in the PHRENO-MAGNET, p. 87.

by my finger in the centre of that region marked on the common busts and charts as *Veneration*, he slowly bent his knees, and raised and then closed his hands in an attitude of the most intense devotion. On my touching his eyelids he began to pray. On touching the region of *Self-Esteem*, after the influence had been dispelled from *Veneration*, he assumed an attitude of great personal consequence ; and on this point of contact being left for that of *Approbativeness*, he began to adonise himself, and to strut about with a consummate air of suavity and complacency. He whistled and sang on the region of *Tune* being operated upon ; under that of *Philo-progenitiveness* dreamed of nursing ; of quarrelling under *Combativeness ;* and so of several others. As the patient was well known by us, and believed to be ignorant of phrenology, these phenomena were considered at the time very satisfactory and conclusive. But as he afterwards exhibited signs of lucidity in such a degree as correctly to describe several articles, especially defining the value and dates of various coins, held over the top of his head by parties standing behind him, the phenomena in this case might possibly admit of explanation on other than phrenological principles. It is, however, to the record of facts, and not the discussion of theories, we are at present devoted.

As time passed on, other evidence of the same character (making allowance, of course, for peculiar idiosyncrasies) became rife enough. By the cottage fire-side, in Sherwood Forest, or in remote Yorkshire valleys, where mesmerism had never been heard of before, and where the parties operated upon did not know the meaning of the word phrenology, I tried the same experiments with analogical results, and found that the most loutish plough-boys, shepherds, smiths, and weavers, could thus have particular faculties so stimulated by these manipulations, as to manifest for the time the most exalted powers of gesticulation, oratory, and song, each according to his natural gift or bent. There was one young man, of the name of

Wilkinson, a penknife cutler, of Sheffield, on whom I operated before Dr. Elliotson, and William and Mary Howitt and other friends, in London, and who in his somniloquence composed the most beautiful poetry, the theme of which might be changed, or modified, in an instant, as I moved my finger from one part of his head to another; and that without inducing the slightest pause, or a fault in the logic, or without injuring the measure or rhyme of the poem in any degree! On touching a point in the region marked in the popular charts as *Ideality*, he began to compose. If, in addition to this, I touched *Philo-progenitiveness*, he would discourse of the beauty, affection, and innocence of infantine life; or, under *Inhabitiveness*, of the scenes of home and of domestic felicity. Under the influence of *Causality*, he would inquire in the most philosophical yet impassioned manner into the origin of nature. Add *Wonder*, and he would penetrate into the dimmest regions of mystery; *Self-esteem*, and he would rhapsodise on the natural dignity of man, and his privilege to explore the vast and the marvellous; *Veneration*, and he would bow with submission, and expatiate on the goodness and majesty, and sufficiency of God; *Hope*, and he would look with delight for communion with supernal intelligences, and sing of Heaven— thus developing the poetry that was in him, as I have known others develope, in an equal degree, their mechanical, oratorical, or histrionic powers. Those who know me and my previous writings, will not wonder that with evidence like this to encourage me, I prosecuted my investigations with increasing vigour and delight.

CHAPTER III.

FURTHER APPARENT CORROBORATIONS OF PHRENOLOGY—CASE OF
REMARKABLE SUSCEPTIBILITY TO EXTERNAL IMPRESSIONS—IN-
DICATIONS OF DISTINCT FACULTIES NOT PREVIOUSLY RECOGNISED.

ONE evening I was trying experiments with Mr. D.
G. Goyder, editor of the *Phrenological Almanac*, and
Mr. Henry Atkin, at the house of the latter intelligent
friend in Sheffield. The patient was an uneducated
girl, who had never been mesmerised before, and if not
totally ignorant of phrenology, could only have caught
of it the most vague popular idea. She was passed
into a deep mesmeric sleep, by me, in about twenty
minutes, in the presence of Mrs. Atkin, and then
brought before the rest of the company without appear-
ing in the least disturbed. On my touching the region
of *Tune*, she broke forth in a strain of melody as sweet
as it was loud and clear; and gave a few equally striking indications of the functions of other faculties. But
something followed that surprised and puzzled us, since
when Mr. Goyder suggested that I should excite her
Imitativeness, and I touched (as it appeared on close scru-
tiny) a point rather towards the back of the space allotted
to that organ, she responded in terms quite at variance
with our anticipation, manifesting diligence or industry in a most significant and powerful manner—but
nothing of imitation. She persisted that she was at
work, not imitating any body, and would not be hin-
dered by our questions and interruptions. This was so
contrary to the suggestions of Mr. Goyder and to my

own anticipation—so opposed to what we understood of
phrenology—as to make us for a time suspend our
judgment; and the patient being awoke, declared herself oblivious of all that had passed in her sleep.

A few days afterwards I met incidentally with a
young man, who had first been mesmerised on Mr.
Braid's plan of staring continuously at some motionless
object, by which he was thrown into a state resembling
an epileptic fit and made so painfully susceptible to
nearly all external influences that the slightest atmo-
spheric changes, as well as the forms and qualities of
the objects he handled, would afterwards affect him
most strangely, although a person of great muscular
energy, firmness, and sagacity. I knew him on one
occasion to be so affected by the mere handling or
presence of a skull, although he was not aware of
the source of the influence, as to become an impersonation of the character of the man to whom it had
belonged. Phrenologically speaking, it must have been
the cranium of one sadly deficient in all the cheerful and
hopeful characteristics of humanity, but given to anger
and to alimentive gratification ; probably drunkenness.
It had been used by Edmund Kean, when representing
Hamlet in a provincial theatre, and was, for that reason,
valued as a relic by the young man to whom I allude,
in whose possession it had been only a few hours, when
he became wretched—despondent to the utmost degree;
out of his usual sympathy with what was good and
beautiful, and, as the evening advanced, delirious, with
a determination to suicide. He could not tell me the
cause of this, nor was I then myself aware of it ; but sat
up with him all night to prevent him carrying his purpose into execution. It was a night of horrors; but I
kept calm and hopeful myself, which with thankfulness I may observe is generally the case where my aid
is likely to be of benefit to a patient, however violent
his paroxysms. Next day, while he was still in a hot
fever, delirious and most wretched, by a mere incident
I detected the cause ; had the noxious object taken

away ; removed his fever, reducing, in a few minutes, the pulse from 120 to 80, by what Deleuze calls the long passes; and he became almost instantaneously well; for which I raised my thoughts to Heaven in gratitude. My firm conviction, founded upon what I have seen in this and other cases, is, that diseases presenting symptoms similar to the foregoing might often be removed by means as simple, if we better understood the connexion between the world without and the world within—external nature as connected with our internal sympathies and antipathies.

> " To every form of being is assign'd
> An active principle, howe'er removed
> From sense and observation; it subsists
> In all things; in all natures; in the stars
> Of azure heaven; the unenduring clouds;
> In flower and tree, and every pebbly stone
> That paves the brook; the stationary rock,
> The moving waters, and the invisible air."

These expressive lines are from Wordsworth, who might, according to the fact stated above, have drawn another illustration even from the grave itself.*

And the question arises as to whether or not self-mesmerism, or " hypotism," does not mainly differ from the common results of " magnetic" manipulation in this, that it sometimes quickens the susceptibility of the patient to external impressions—to the influence of inanimate objects—without supplying or generating the additional animal force necessary for sustaining him in his new condition. But to proceed.

Finding this young man so susceptible that I could either quicken or suspend sensation in any part of his body—could, in fact, lock or unlock his jaw by operating upon his toes even—I thought that, with judicious treatment, he would be a good subject for phreno-mesmerism; and so I found him, always corroborating the doctrines of Gall when I attempted to " magnetise"

---

* For many curious illustrations of this and other mysterious principles, read THE SEERESS OF PREVORST, translated by Mrs. Crowe. London: J. C. Moore, 1845.

the brain by touching the *centre* of those spaces given
by that philosopher to the organs he had discovered.
One day, however, on my touching, as I thought, the
region of *Imitativeness*, he commenced with great energy
the same movements of his hands as those required in
the trade he worked at—that of a file-cutter. Thinking
this might be really a manifestation of Imitativeness, I
asked him what he was doing. His reply was, " Why,
don't you see? Cutting files, to be sure. Don't bother
me." " Who have you seen cutting files?" was my next
question. " Why, don't you see that I am cutting them
myself ?" was his reply. " Well," I continued, " but
why are you cutting them?" " Because," said he, " they
are wanted, and if you hinder me in this way, I shan't
be able to get them done soon enough." At the close
of this parley, my finger-end accidentally slipped a little
forward, when he began to manifest imitation by mock-
ing every sound that was made. The above indication
of diligence, it should be remembered, resulted from
my exciting the same part in this patient as in Mr.
Atkin's servant; but, in both cases, altogether independent of my anticipation: in the first, in opposition
to a direct verbal suggestion; and, in the second, in opposition to the patient's own ideas of phrenology.

The thought now struck me, that as most if not all
of the other functions had been so accurately and
strikingly indicated in these cases that it would require
any one who might attempt to simulate them to be at
least a Combe in phrenology, a Locke in metaphysics,
and a Garrick in acting ; since the patients were too
little educated to be more than passive subjects in the
matter—and especially as this manifestation of diligence or industry was not less striking and characteristic of some distinct function than were the indications of those faculties already recognised—Mr.
La Roy Sunderland might possibly be correct in his
hypothesis of a great amplification, and that what I now
saw was the natural language of the moral faculty of
Diligence, the organ of which might be seated in that

part of the head. Acting upon this idea, and avoiding
as much a possible any design or suggestion as to the
results, I afterwards proceeded, by minute changes of
the point of contact, over the entire head of this patient,
and the heads of others in the same way ; some of my
friends and correspondents have done the same with similar results; and I am bound to state my conviction, that if
such results are corroborative of phrenology at all, they
are equally so of a very great amplification of its de-
tails.* If, however, they can be referred with more
certainty and satisfaction to any other principle, nothing
will afford me more pleasure than to give way to it.
A pioneer and expositor, rather than a theorist, I wish
my opinions to be valued only according to the facts
upon which they are founded. I am well aware, and
have sometimes shown how, in certain conditions of
the patients, similar results may be obtained by verbal suggestion, or association of ideas with particular
points of contact in any part of the body, so that they
may be *trained* to whistle or sing if we touch the nose,
and to weep with compassion if we touch the heel or the
elbow. I am also well aware of, and shall proceed to
describe some beautiful cases of silent mental communion between operator and patient, by which the
mute intention or expectation of one is indicated by
the words or actions of the other. But how are we to
explain those phenomena arising with such consistency
—after a due allowance for idiosyncratic differences has
been made—from what appears to be the paramount
action of particular faculties, when they are opposed
alike to the anticipations of the operator, the opinions of
the patient, and the verbal suggestions of bystanders,
if we do not recognise the hypothesis of a special influence through a distinct organic medium? For the
present I leave this question with the reader.

* See various articles on the subject by myself, Mr. Stenson, and
others, in THE PHRENO-MAGNET, (Simpkin and Marshall), 1843; and
in the PHRENOLOGICAL ALMANAC, (Goyder, Glasgow), 1845.

CHAPTER IV.

INFLUENCE OF THE AUTHOR'S EXPERIENCE UPON HIS OWN MIND—
LAWS OF SYMPATHY AND COINCIDENCE—STRIKING INSTANCE—
MESMERIC ILLUSTRATIONS.

IN proportion as my knowledge of mesmerism advanced, and my faith and practice became more confirmed, my powers seemed to be strengthened, exalted and refined. So startling, however, at times were the views that burst upon me, as to cause me almost to falter in my steps, as if on the threshold of a forbidden world. Still there was seldom long wanting some incident to guide and encourage me to a point at which what had at first been strange and mysterious became familiar and clear. Thus it was that I could at last observe my own silent will or anticipation responded to by another—in vigilance often as well as in sleep—without any compunction, though not without a feeling of solemnity, and a deep and increasing sense of *my own responsibility for the consequences*. And after all, is there (except that we perceive them in a new light), any thing so very novel in these facts themselves? Perhaps it is only because we have not thought sufficiently of the common laws of sympathy and coincidence that they surprise us in the least. Without being mesmerised at all by special manipulations, how often do we think of persons who are approaching before they come into sight! Has not one of the most familiar proverbs arisen out of this fact? How often, too, we simultaneously write or start the same ideas in conversation,

although unable to find their origin in our previous
discourse, or to refer them to any other obvious
motive!   My own recollection would furnish me with
a volume of examples—so perhaps would that of almost
any other equally observant person.   I have a friend
who is remarkably subject to this kind of experience;
and on one occasion he gave me the following striking
illustration of it:—

" I was (says he) when at Ackworth School, in
Yorkshire, warmly attached to another boy of my own
age, with whom I used to ramble, and to read and
converse on every topic in which we could be mu-
tually interested, and to whom I sometimes also spoke
of my presentiments regarding our future career.   At
the age of fourteen we were separated, and neither of
us for more than ten years heard what had become of
the other.   At length I became a traveller, and was
one day contemplating with a solemn yet ecstatic feeling the Falls of Niagara, in the neighbourhood of which
also were scattered several other parties similarly engaged.   As I continued to gaze, a gleam of sunshine
stole athwart one particular part of the scene with an
effect that thrilled me with wonder and delight.   I
thought, whilst looking upon it, of my early reading
and hopes ; my wanderings with my friend, and our
conversations on the beauty and grandeur of nature;
and much did I marvel what had become of him, and
wish that he could then participate in my exalted enjoyment.   From this reverie I was at length startled by
some one coming towards me from behind, and was
turning round with the intent of directing his attention
to the point of interest I have named.   He had, however, already seen it, and was advancing towards me
for the same purpose, animated by the same feeling,
the same recollections and associations ; and, sure
enough, it was the identical man at the moment occu-
pying my own thoughts—my old schoolfellow who, like
myself, had become a traveller; and thus, influenced
by one motive, we met at the Falls of Niagara, more

than 3000 miles from Yorkshire, after years of fruitless inquiry for intelligence of each other. What is still more remarkable, we met three times afterwards in different parts of the world under circumstances equally peculiar and unlooked for!"

All such occurrences as the foregoing have usually been explained upon the principle of coincidence; but mesmerism has taught me that there may be in it something more than mere chance, which those who use the term generally mean. Coincidence itself may have laws as regular and determinate as they are subtle ; and are not the following simple mesmeric incidents calculated in some slight degree to elucidate them?

Being called one day to an intelligent young lady, in a very delicate state of health, and who had first been mesmerised by a female friend, I found her so susceptible that I had only to *will* her to be somnolent and she almost immediately became so. Then, whatever I did ideally she represented actually, even to the extent of conversing with one of her acquaintance, who was not present. I thought of creation, Providence, and prayer, when she knelt most gracefully, and lifted her hands in silent adoration. Then of firmness and independence, when she arose and assumed the appropriate attitude of lofty determination. I next willed that she should approach and shake hands with me, which was scarcely accomplished when, on changing my mood to one of scorn, she turned away and looked indignant. Benignity and other sentiments in myself, were all represented with equal truthfulness by her ; until, at last, indulging in a feeling of sober cheerfulness, in which of course she joined, I awoke her from the trance by gentle wafting, when she was utterly oblivious of all that had occurred. On a subsequent occasion, she described occurrences at the moment they were transpiring at a great distance, which in due course were proved to have been exactly accordant with her words ; and she even went so far as to divine my very thoughts with accuracy. This was altogether without any observable organic excitement.

Another case, is that of a young man, at the time he was influenced perfectly vigilant. It was about the season of the bursting of buds and the early twitterings of building birds, with a half-misty, half-sunny and balmy atmosphere, that I rode with him one morning from York to Knaresborough, in company with others, all very susceptible, though variously so, to mesmeric influences. The beauty and quiet of the scenery and the time ; the greening pastures and smiling river glimpses; the bank-sides at hand just ready to flush into floweriness, and the woods afar to rush into foliage, all inspired me with admiration, love, and hope, awaking veneration and adoration into glowing activity; and I mused delightedly yet reverentially on the beauties, wonders, and mysteries of creation. A sudden burst upon me of the valley of the Nidd with its manifold charms had given an additional stimulus to these feelings, and on retiring to our little room at the inn, as we all sat together, I felt an unusual clearness and expansiveness yet subjection of spirit, like that described by the primitive Quakers in their meetings, and which I have sometimes experienced, too, when communing deeply with great poets.

During this melting and ecstatic flow of feeling on my own part, to which I gave little or no verbal utterance, the young man in question on a sudden looked wistfully towards me, and begged I would not think him silly; but something, he said, like a slight electric spark had thrilled the upper portion of his brain, had extended its influence over his whole system, and he believed he should be compelled to kneel down, without being able to explain the cause, except that an unusual reverential feeling accompanied the impulse. I was startled, but said nothing to him of my thoughts, and began to muse on the laws of sympathy. Only a short time had passed in this mood, when he exclaimed,

" How strange! *It* has come again, but on the side of my head (pointing to the region of *Adhesiveness*), and you must excuse me, but I feel forced to come to you;" and he was leaning towards me from his chair, when I suddenly changed my mood to one of pure beneficence. Here he threw himself back; the kindliest smile uplit his whole face; and, with one hand on his breast and the other stretched out, he said he felt " as though he could love all mankind at once;" and the influence had fallen this time on the front of his head and in his bosom! This youth was an uneducated stocking-weaver, a native of Ireland, at that time all but entirely ignorant of phrenology.

A different yet analogous illustration of the principle of mental communion was, on another occasion, afforded me by a man in the mesmeric sleep. During a public lecture in the course of the evening he had given several most decided indications of lucidity—describing with accuracy many places it was pretty evident he had not visited or had described to him by others. From the lecture we were accompanied by a medical gentleman who had acted as chairman, and who was desirous of further evidence in private. The patient having been again mesmerised, as he sat between us we began to try upon him a series of experiments in phreno-mesmerism. The conditions were that no organ should be named by either of us except silently, in writing, upon a slip of paper, to be carefully passed from one to the other of us *behind* him: so that it was impossible he could receive a suggestion, even though his eyes had been open, especially as it was arranged that I should excite the different faculties our visiter might promiscuously name by pointing my finger to the head *without actual contact*. To all these operations the patient responded with the greatest facility and accuracy—becoming more susceptible and clear as the experiments proceeded, until he distinctly *read* the papers as they were handed past the *back* of his head, and soon afterwards gave with intense effect the natural language of any organ my coadjutor thought of, even before he had time to write the name of it! In this case, and on the same occasion, other and still more beautiful and striking phenomena were educed; but to a world so sceptical I scarcely feel justified in giving them publication yet— although no dream, but matters of actual experience that can never be obliterated from that page on which our existence itself is written—the book of Nature, the language of which is *facts*. They relate to prevision, premonition, prophecy, and other principles, founded, as I think, in man's spirituality. But let me not awaken prejudice.

CHAPTER V.

Public Lectures, Lecturers, and their Traducers—The Ene-
mies of Mesmerism compose the very Class to which some
would confine its Practice—Popular Treatment of the
Question contrasted with the Conduct of some in Select
Circles—The Right of "the Common People" to a Knowledge of its Powers.

The scribes and pharisees of Judea, in the days of
old, would have excluded "the common people" (notwithstanding their openness to receive the truth with
gladness) from the blessings of religion; and the scientific scribes and pharisees of modern England have
shown precisely the same disposition with regard to
mesmerism. When I hear any one say a word against
popular lecturing on mesmerism, I invariably ask if he
or she be in circumstances, or endowed with the requisite powers, to command esteem in the same walk. If
such people, when they are denouncing us, would just
" suppose a change of cases," they would probably be
led to modify their tone. I know, and regret it as
deeply as any one, that there are ignorant quacks and
impostors in mesmerism, the same as in medicine and
even in religion—men whose acts would stain any
cause—yet, on the other hand, I know some lecturers
on this subject whose conduct would raise and ennoble
any profession that had truth for its basis, as mesmerism has. But it is said that by bringing the more
beautiful and subtle phenomena of mesmerism before
crowds, we are throwing " pearls before swine," and

into the lap of the ignorant an instrument that might be used for base and unholy purposes. In reply to this I would ask, *who are the wise?* To what class and profession do the Wakleys, and Radclyffe Halls, and Headlam Greenhows belong? Is the editor of the *Athenæum* a specimen of " mind among the spindles," or hard and impervious to truth as the spindle itself? Miss Martineau and other well-meaning writers should have weighed these things before so unmercifully and indiscriminately condemning the whole class of lecturers. Not that I am blind to all possibility of evil, but because there has been too much special pleading against us is it that I advert to these points with somewhat of earnestness—it may seem of severity; but benevolence and a hope for the best accompany the allusion. Do we put out the domestic fire because Moscow was destroyed, or because some incendiary may have burnt our neighbour's house? We educate even children to use it properly, and then trust them with it as we would ourselves. So we may the people with mesmerism. Indeed, immense volumes might be filled with instances of the beneficial use of mesmerism by " the common people," who obtained the elements of their knowledge from public lecturers; yet quite as much might be said, on the other side, of the insult and misrepresentation to which its advocates have been subjected by the literary and scientific magnates of the day; and that not merely in popular lecture-halls but in hospitals, colleges, dignified societies, and even in private drawing-rooms. Further: there is not on record, so far as I am aware, a single instance of its criminal abuse by one of the common—that is, of the working—people. One of the professional railers against Miss Martineau did allude, in a most indelicate spirit, to some case of the kind. But who was the reputed criminal ? A PHYSICIAN! " The church-yards tell no tales," says a shrewd old proverb; but there are and have been doctors and other learned men with much to answer for in the world to come; and it would be quite as rational because of this to denounce the whole of the medical profession, in which there are several of the noblest spirits of the age, as, for the forestated reasons, to run down " the common people" and the lecturers by whom they love to be instructed when nobody else attempts to instruct them.

My becoming a lecturer on mesmerism was as simply a matter of course as my becoming an inquirer. In the summer of 1842, when on a tour among the mountains of Derbyshire, I descended one evening to the inn at Castleton to rest, when mesmerism chancing to be a subject of conversation, I was asked what I knew of it, and in reply mentioned some of the occurrences already related in this book. Several of the friendly people present, being much interested by what they heard, desired me to come again and give them a lecture with experimental illustrations. On reaching home I named the subject to Mr. Rodgers, who consented to accompany me on what appeared so curious yet pleasant an excursion, and our meeting was fixed for a Saturday evening. A small but fashionable party attended from Buxton, with several of the townspeople, and the experiments were satisfactory. Still I had no idea of becoming a professional lecturer till, in the month of November of the same year, a similar request was made by the committee of the Sheffield Mechanics' Institution, and the result not only astounded me, but appeared completely to revolutionise my destiny, and to give at the time an impulse to mesmerism that was felt through the country.

My first public lecture in Sheffield was in the large assembly-room where M. La Fontaine's experiments had been previously given. There was little need now to resort to the old tests. Operator and subjects operated on being so well known in the town, and so many of the townspeople having experimented for themselves, the room was filled with hundreds who came to believe and learn, and hundreds went away unable to gain admission. To remedy this difficulty, the Amphitheatre was engaged by the committee for another lecture; but even that large building was filled from the stage to the roof, it is supposed, by not less than three thousand people, and again more than a thousand who came were unable to gain admission—when yet another lecture followed in which an equal interest was taken.

In York and Nottingham, where I was equally well known, having formerly been in both places connected with the press, a similar desire was evinced to see the experiments, and not less interest manifested in the results. Doctors and educators who came to oppose remained to approve. Not less than three hundred other experimenters came publicly before the country; and it was utterly impossible for some of them, under the circumstances, again to retire into their original privacy.

Since then I have experimented, by invitation, in almost every large town from London to Dundee. In the most fashionable and aristocratic, as well as in the most grave, scientific circles, the phenomena have been viewed with all the gradations of regard, from intense rational delight down to a meaningless quiz, a shrug, or a simper. But I am bound to say, after all I have experienced, that in no rank of society have I ever seen a more intense yet quiet and philosophical interest evinced in mesmerism, than by some of the large popular audiences in the manufacturing towns of Yorkshire and Lancashire, and other districts of the middle and north of England and Scotland. Do not let me be misunderstood: it would be impossible to think but with the deepest respect cf the kindly and unostentatious regard shown for mesmerism on various occasions by men famous in science, and by families of high aristocratic distinction. But in my estimation "the common people" of England and Scotland rank very high for humanity and intelligence, when their behaviour is compared with that of some in the class to which several writers would have mesmerism confined! How beautiful it was, in one town, to see the Vicar acting as chairman, and the lecture-theatre filled with nearly a thousand of his parishioners of all ranks, all animated by one kindly spirit of observation and inquiry, as fact after fact was laid before them under circumstances that rendered deception on one side or suspicion on the other quite impossible; whilst I endeavoured to show the analogy of the different states exhibited to the various conditions of health and disease, and the power that mesmerism gives us to regulate and control them. At another place, where the clergyman allowed me in the presence of a large meeting to test the influence upon his own son; whilst, listened to with the profoundest attention, I explained its uses and laid down infallible rules for preventing its abuse. At another where, in presence of the Mayor and seven hundred of the inhabitants, the free and healthy use of a contracted leg was restored to one of the citizens by a mesmeric experiment, without pain, after all other means had failed; and where public evidence was given by the patients themselves of its efficacy in the cure of deafness, lumbago, paralysis, stammering, inflammations, swellings of the ancles, and many other complaints. In the north of Scotland, where a distinguished philosopher (as chairman) gave his testimony to the validity of a class of facts that awoke such interest in the neighbourhood as could not subside, and where mesmerism has since been continually used as a curative or palliative of the most grievous disorders. And again, in a midland English town, where, owing to there being no good instrumental music at hand by which I might illustrate the influence of melody upon the system in the mesmeric trance,—when the soul beams so brightly through the countenance and the whole body moves or basks in such perfect and ecstatic harmony with the sounds,—the entire audience accorded, as with one voice, in a sweet expressive tune that drew forth some of the sublimest and most instructive psychical phenomena they had ever contemplated. Contrast these facts—popular and incontrovertible facts—with the represented or misrepresented failures and puerile bickerings so often attending or following experiments in exclusive circles; and then, ye who consider yourselves of " the higher walk of mesmerists," tell me why a Yorkshire weaver or a Northamptonshire peasant has less right than you to participate in such knowledge. Do astronomers and botanists alone enjoy or receive instruction from the stars or the flowers? Has none but the physician ever relieved pain? Do none but priests smooth the death-bed pillow? A time came when Dives would have been glad of the friendship even of Lazarus. Think of these things, and speak not contemptuously of " the common people."

CHAPTER VI.

Mesmeric Results not to be confounded with Miracles—
Reasons for believing in the Transmission of Health, as
well as of Disease, by Contagion—Illustrative Cases introduced.

It is a maxim, that there is not in nature a single
agent without a use proportionate to its power. One
of the principal uses of mesmerism, pathetism, or vital
magnetism, is doubtless the correction of vital derangements. So striking have been some of its effects
in this way as to cause many to regard it as a sort of
scientific divinity, and to consider it the parent of all
the attested miracles of both modern and ancient times:
a view, as it appears to me, very erroneous, and from
which I therefore unequivocally express my dissent.
Subtle and potent though it be, and useful as enabling
us to cultivate our benevolence and other humane
faculties in the relief of our brother, or friend, or
neighbour by applying it to his ailments, we have yet
the best authority for regarding this influence as altogether subordinate to that Power which, being adequate
in the first instance to the creation of the world, still
occasionally manifests its superiority to those laws by
which in ordinary the world is governed. If we are
to believe history, the magicians of old understood much
more of magnetic practice—could see deeper into
the nature of themselves, and work many more wonders than are witnessed in our day. One of them, a
Persian, who lived on the mountain overlooking Taoces,

was himself, at one period of his life, almost continuously lucid or clairvoyant. Yet, mark how a number
of these sages—" *wise men from the East*"*—came to
the BABE IN BETHLEHEM, and acknowledged the in-
feriority of their influence to that of pure, unostentatious, and comprehensive Christianity! True, since
Jesus did not disdain to use even dirt and spittle as
agents, and since he felt " a virtue gone out of him"
on an occasion when another was benefitted by touching him, I would not deny that, as Lord of All, he
might use magnetism, or any other agent in creation, for
the working out of his compassionate designs. And
when he commanded his humble followers to *heal the
sick* as well as to preach the Gospel, I do not deny
that he was bidding them to use an agent as natural
and common to them all as the language in which they
were to preach. As he came to teach that religion was not confined to the priests and pharisees,
but belonged as well to the common people ; so
also he showed that the powers of nature were not alone
in the hands of the magicians or men of science—of
whom the exclusive doctors in our day, who blindly
deny the use of mesmerism whilst the people are curing
each other by it, afford, perhaps, a distant semblance.
But I do not believe that any one can possess the divine
influence He and his Apostles of that or any subsequent
time have manifested, except in proportion as he may
become *renewed* and live the same obedient, unselfish,
pure, faithful, divine life they lived and enjoined. If
man were fully to comply with this, instead of belying
what is divine by his hypocrisy or denying it by his
scepticism, it is impossible for us to tell the extent of knowledge and power he would possess, as no doubt it would
be commensurate with his faith and purity. Christianity
is more than a sun in the firmament; compared with it
science is no more than a lamp in a cloister. Whilst
we remain shut up in this cloister of the senses, we are
permitted to learn a little by the lamp if we will; yet

* *Magician* simply means *wise man.*

let us not, by extolling its brilliancy too much, draw attention from a light more primitive, pure, and universal; but " give unto Cæsar the things that are Cæsar's, and unto God the things that are God's."

If we had as much faith in the good as in the evil of our lot, a curative affluence from a healthy body would never have been doubted. We believe in the transmission of disease by contagion; and since nature is as equitable as economical, why not also in the transmission of health? If we have the power of communicating fever, cholera, and small-pox, by our mere presence, without contact—if the plague, sent a thousand miles in a letter from a city where it is already raging, shall on the letter being opened begin new ravages and depopulate another city—what becomes of the doctrine of nature's equitability if we have not the countervailing power, that of communicating health by an analogous law? This should be considered by those who, within sight of ships kept in quarantine for weeks or months, ridicule the means used by mesmerists as idle mummery!

The following cases will illustrate this doctrine, as well as others to which I may allude in passing.

CASE I.—" LITTLE HENRY."

The interesting somnambulist, Henry Wigston, is well known to most of my friends by the above *soubriquet*, having become warmly attached to and been with me for months together, during the past two years. When I first saw him he was errand-boy in a barber's shop, and appeared very poorly and dull, his stature being that of a child of seven or eight years rather than a youth of thirteen (which he then was); his temperament lymphatic; his eyes heavy; and his movements slow. He had not since his infancy been free from a serious affection of the brain, and says he could never play like other boys, for at every attempt

to run or leap, he suffered from a violent and painful
" knocking" or throbbing in his head. He had twice
been mesmerised before having heard of the process;
once by looking intently at a clergyman, preaching
in St. Mary's church, Leicester; and once by fixing his
eyes upon the head of a nail, whilst riding in a cart.
In both instances he was carried home under the supposition that he was " in a fit," and relieved by having
cold water poured upon his head. It is since being mesmerised by me that he has seen the analogy; and I am
well convinced, after devoting much attention to the
subject, that many forms of disease are but what are
termed mesmeric states, unconsciously, or at all events
unintentionally induced, and may be easily cured on
mesmeric principles as the people are made more
familiar with the practice.*

It was Henry's peculiar indications of susceptibility
that first made me offer to mesmerise him, to which
both his master and himself assented after I had explained to them its meaning. In ten minutes from the
commencement of my manipulations the little fellow
was somnambulent, and although he was declared to
know nothing of phrenology, that evening, on being
mesmerised again, he presented one of the most interesting cases of phreno-mesmerism I had seen. The
next day he was perfectly lucid, and described the
internal structure and economy of the human frame,
and the diseases of several strange parties with whom
he was brought into proximity, as clearly and correctly
as could have been done by a regular professor of anatomy—making allowance, of course, for his ignorance
of technicalities. This faculty of lucidity he continued
to exercise with beautiful clearness and certainty—saying that not only human bodies, but many other things

---

* A gentleman of rank and great influence, residing near Sheffield,
writes me that, acting upon this suggestion, he recalled a patient
very easily from a violent hysteric fit by the ordinary process of
" demesmerising." A physician near Huddersfield told me he had
done the same in a case of epilepsy. I shall have more to say on
this subject in a future work.

opaque to us, were *transparent* to him—until one evening a " man of science," who was fond of conjuring, and who afterwards excused himself on the vulgar pretence that he wanted to discover " where the trick lay," inasmuch as he was sceptical, took an opportunity of influencing the boy without my knowledge. This took away his lucidity. For some time afterwards whenever somnambulent he complained of having " net-work over his eyes," and although he yet can read and run about and occasionally give the prognosis of a disease whilst in the sleep, he is by no means so lucid as before. Still he is a most interesting case. In the presence of the Society for the Investigation of Mesmeric Phenomena, during the passing summer, his intellects appeared so exalted and clear as to excite the wonder and delight of every one. His disquisition on the laws of sympathy, coincidence and correspondence, was a perfect masterpiece of ratiocination—and for an uneducated boy, marvellous. There was a poetical beauty too in some of his instantaneous replies to the metaphysical questions poured in upon him that charmed us all. " Henry," said the editor of the *Critic*, " what is thought?" Without a moment's pause he turned his head and quietly replied, " Thought?—thought is silent speaking." Once, when he was mesmerised by a lady, she taught him to play a tune on the pianoforte whilst somnambulent. After being awoke he went to the instrument and played the same again without remembering how he learnt it, yet still feeling as though it had been suggested to him. How often have we a similar feeling in common life! Whence does it come if not from the world of dreams?

On another occasion when in the sleep he was taught to translate some words of Hebrew, but he has no knowledge of them whatever when awake; yet when again in the same state he remembers them well.*

* It is a curious and interesting fact that most mesmeric patients remember when in the sleep—when the external senses are inactive and the inner powers more manifest—what has occurred to

But it is when under the influence of music that
Henry presents the most beautiful mesmeric phenomena.
In answer to sweet sounds his whole body discourses correspondent yet silent music—the poetry of form and
motion! Suspend the music in the middle of a strain,
and his motion also becomes suspended: he is a rigid
and statue-like impersonation of the last sentiment or
passion excited, until his attitude becomes changed
again by a renewal of the melody.*

In speaking of some experiments we had at the house
of Mr. William Howitt, that popular and impressive
writer says of him—" He is thrown in a few seconds,
by mere contact of the hands, into the mesmeric
sleep, and in this responds to many phrenologic touches
in the most beautiful and extraordinary manner. The
effects produced on him by music are in particular
striking. They throw him into attitudes corresponding
to the sentiment of the piece played, which could only
be acquired by a first-rate actor after long and arduous
practice, if they could be reached at all, and which
would form the finest models for the sculptor or painter.
His countenance undergoes equal changes, and at times
acquires a pathos, a tenderness, a sublimity, or an expression of fun, that are singularly beautiful. Several
pieces were played by a German gentleman present,
which he could not possibly have heard before, but to

them in their ordinary life; and by which their mesmeric condition
indeed is much influenced; though when awake, and their external
senses are all active, they are entirely oblivious of what was done by
them when in the inner state. May not this help to show us how
probable it is, that whilst in this external life of sense we do not
understand the soul, circumstances as they pass may still be so photo-
graphed upon and imbue it as to influence it by their effects even
when the senses are laid aside in death? There is something analogous to the idea in my own experience. I was once near the point
of death by drowning. At that moment all that I had been, felt, known,
or done, seemed present to me, as if concentrated in one vivid idea.
Might not this be a glimpse of the opening of the " book of life" in
which all my actions had been noted? I have since read in the works
of De Quincy, " The Opium Eater," of some one else having had a
similar experience—unless it is my own case he has related.
    * The tasteful and ingenious artist, Henry Collen, Esq., of Lon-
don, has taken excellent sketches of some of these attitudes.

the spirit of which he responded in the most inimitable manner, being sunk into sadness, raised into holy adoration, and kindled in an energy of martial or patriotic ardour, accompanied by the finest correspondent attitudes and action. His faculty of imitation being tested, he threw back any sound issuing from the company as the most perfect echo would do, as a rock or a wall having the power to fling back sound would do. He was addressed in various languages, and threw back every sentence with the most perfect pronunciation, and generally without the omission of a single syllable. While the company were occupied in conversation on this matter, and he was left standing unobserved by the majority, those who had kept their attention upon him perceived to their astonishment that he continued to reflect all mixed and multiform sounds that arose from their conversation. It was now a strange murmur, now a clear utterance of a sentence, as some one spoke out louder and more distinct than the rest. Coughs, laughs, and even a low whistle, introduced by a silent watcher of him, all had their place in these curious responses."

In one of his somnambulic states, he can be made upon the slightest suggestion to dream, and the dream may be modified as we please, either by special phrenological excitement or by further verbal suggestions. Sometimes he has thus been made to impersonate a town-crier, when on his *Philo-progenitiveness* being excited he would cry a child lost—under *Combativeness* a prize-fight or a debate —under *Cautiousness* a warning to trespassers—under *Veneration* and *Benevolence* a charity sermon to be preached; and all these announcements might be modified or varied as other organs were brought co-relatively into action; and these results are so instantaneous, and so perfectly natural and logical withal, as to render the supposition of mere acting in the case quite impossible. His impersonation of a locomotive steam-engine is not less accurate—his imitation both of the motions and sounds, complex as they are, giving the most beautiful and striking ideal that any thing beside the machine itself when active could convey.

Sometimes I have thrown one hemisphere of his brain, and the corresponding side of his body into an abnormal and quiescent state by passes, and preserved the perfect normality and activity of the other. The same might be done with any particular limb, or any specific portion of it. The part thus affected would be quite numbed or rigid, yet there would be no apparent tendency to sleep, or any interference with the functions of the parts not thus specifically acted upon. At one time I could make him feel warm when cold, or cool and refreshed when thirsty, by a few passes, and produce any medicinal effect I wished upon his body by giving him water with a curative intention: but latterly there has been little or no occasion for the practice, and I do not think a very frequent repetition of such experiments advisable where no specific benefit can be derived from them. They are, however, occasionally interesting as illustrative of very important principles and powers.

Such are many of the curious phenomena presented by this case; and now methinks I hear some timid reader inquire if these experiments have produced no injurious effects on the boy, to which I answer, so far as it is possible to judge from appearances, quite the contrary. It is true that, however frequent some of the experiments may have been, they have always been conducted by me in the most careful manner; and though often in the presence of a public audience, not less with a view to the patient's benefit; and the consequence is that his head which daily ached and throbbed before he was mesmerised, is never now in pain at all. His eye which was dim and heavy is bright and active. His temperament that was so lymphatic is becoming fibrous. His stature so stunted, has improved more, I am told, in the two years he has known me than in the five preceding years; and, except for a cold he has recently taken through his own inadvertance, he] appears altogether as well and strong as the paternal regard I feel for him could make me wish.

CASE II.—CURE OF HYSTERIA.

James Knight, Esq. and Mr. Mason, surgeon, of Burton-on-Trent, introduced me, in October, 1843, to a highly respectable and intellectual lady, who for twenty years had been subject to hysteria, in its worst form, and had spent an exceedingly large sum of money in medicine, without relief. For some time not a day had passed without a series of distressing paroxysms, and she had consented to try mesmerism—not that she had the slightest faith in it, but because of having tried every other reputed specific to no purpose, she wished to have the satisfaction of knowing that she had not neglected herself in this. Of the gentlemen who introduced me, one—Mr. Knight—was a firm believer in the efficacy of mesmerism; he is, in fact, one of its most enthusiastic, benevolent, and successful practisers; but Mr. Mason at the time had no faith in it at all, yet as the *last chance* in the patient's case, he was desirous of seeing it tried, saying that if it cured her he should certainly admit its great usefulness; for, since she was of a strong and somewhat philosophical mind whatever might be the reduction of her physical powers, it would be wrong to attribute any change merely to what is often miscalled the imagination.

It has long been my belief, that as by inoculation we bring on a premature crisis of some disorders of the grosser animal juices—as in small-pox or measles for instance—and thus assist nature in getting rid altogether of the virus; so, where there is a constitutional tendency to maladies more purely nervous, we may by mesmerism hasten a crisis in them, and by an analogous law prevent their recurrence in a more distressing form. In one case we impregnate the blood with ponderable matter scarcely less gross than itself, and in the other case, by an agent more refined, we influence the im-

D

ponderable fluid constituting those vital forces by which our normal motions are regulated, and the derangement of which occasions those convulsions and tremors incident to some of the more subtle forms of disease. With this idea, I begged of the patient not to be uneasy whatever might transpire, but to submit quietly and let the influence have its own effect. In about eight minutes, whilst I was pursuing my manipulations, her breathing appeared affected. At about the twelfth minute there was an occurrence of the kind of paroxysms to which she was ordinarily subject. These I allowed to go on for a short time, and then concentrating my will upon the purpose,—using soothing passes with my hands downwards, over the face and chest, and afterwards gently taking hold of her own hands with the same idea,—I changed her condition to one of perfect serenity, and after a few more passes awoke her from what appeared to be a conscious sleep;—for though she could not open her eyes, she was perfectly aware of her state and could reason upon it, or answer any of my questions with the greatest facility. When recovered she could remember and describe all she had undergone, but said there was now complete freedom from the exhaustion that invariably followed her ordinary paroxysms. At the next *séance* she was mesmerised in a much shorter period, the paroxysms were more feeble, and her refreshment greater on being awoke. On the third occasion she had scarcely any paroxysms at all, was thrown into ecstacy by music, and awoke still better. Thus she went on improving at every *séance* until the eighth, when on my awaking her, she declared that she felt quite well—as she was wont to feel twenty years before, but as she had never felt in the interim! I gave instructions to one of her female friends how to proceed with her, should there be any return of the complaint, and left the town. Some months afterwards, Mr. Knight wrote me that she continued perfectly well, and that they were all thankful for mesmerism. More than a year afterwards, the lady herself favoured me with a friendly and gratifying letter, in which she said there had then been no return whatever of her disorder, although before I mesmerised her she had not for years been a day without some appearance of its painful symptoms.*

CASE III.—EPILEPSY AT HALIFAX.

In February, 1844, I visited Halifax, where a " Medical Commission for the Investigation of Mesmeric Phenomena" was instituted, and many experiments, of a most convincing character, were tried at the Philosophical Hall.† At one of our meetings, a girl, subject to daily attacks of epilepsy, was introduced, for the purpose of being operated upon. She knew nothing of mesmerism; and, though attended by her mother, on seeing so many medical men, she was evidently fearful of some severe operation, and so resisted the tendency to sleep resulting from my manipulations. She asserted, in fact, that she was not influenced at all; but on leaving the room fell into a sound sleep, from which no ordinary measures could awake her. This one of her family came in a state of

* On mentioning this case in one of my lectures, a medical practitioner got up and endeavoured to invalidate its effect upon the audience by saying, that " it was *only* a case of hysteria, the symptoms of which were merely results of the imagination ; and that he was quite willing to let mesmerism have the full benefit of such cases, since the Faculty were well aware how *useless* it was to treat them medically !" My reply was, that he could not have paid the profession a worse compliment than by the remark ; for if what he said were true (which, however, I denied *in toto*), those who had been for nearly twenty years receiving fees from the lady for medicine, *knowing it to be useless*, might as well have robbed her—since *the loss of her money*, at all events, *was not imaginary*. The doctor was silent.

† It is worth recording, as a feature of the age, that a physician of fashionable practice in the town, on being invited to assist in this investigation, protested against it altogether in the most contemptuous terms, on the ground that the fallacy of mesmerism was too apparent to permit him to entertain the thought that it needed inquiry at all ; in short, that any such inquiry would be disgraceful to the profession!

alarm to tell us, and, accompanied by Dr. Inglis, I went to her immediately, and soon restored her by one of the simple processes of " demesmerising," namely, wafting her briskly with a silken handkerchief.

At our next meeting she was again operated upon, and presented several of the ordinary somnolent and other phenomena. Subsequently Dr. Inglis (a physician of very superior intelligence and skill, residing in the town,) mesmerised her occasionally, and some months afterwards I was informed that there had not been any recurrence of her paroxysms.

CASE IV.—CURE OF HEADACHE AND NAUSEA.

AGNES RANDY, domestic servant to Mr. Edward Charlton, bookseller of Newcastle-upon-Tyne, came to me on the 21st of June, 1844, having been afflicted with a violent headache and sickness every morning and evening for a year and a half, during which time she had been treated by several of the Faculty without advantage. Having made passes over the head and stomach, and given her mesmerised water occasionally, she had gone on improving from the first interview until the 29th of the month, when she came to me for the last time, and declared herself quite well.

CASE V.—CURE OF TIC-DOLOUREUX.

About the period of the foregoing case, the lady of an officer in the customs at Newcastle came to me, under a grievous attack of *tic-doloureux*, and was cured by downward passes over the head and face, without the accompaniment of sleep, or even of the slightest drowsiness. I have had three or four other similar cases: so has Dr. G. C. Holland, having given, by the same simple means, permanent relief to one of my own intimate friends after other measures had failed.

Case VI.—Spinal Affection Cured.

JOHN M'WILLIAMS, cotton-spinner, Caldew-gate, Carlisle, aged thirty-four, had been ill nine weeks of a bilious attack, ending in an affection of the spine, which made it painful for him to walk, and, in short, nearly suspended all power in his lower limbs. He had been under the treatment of two of the Faculty, was cupped, and took a great variety of medicine, but without any beneficial effect. He came to me on the 7th of August, 1844, when I made passes over his back and legs, whilst he remained in a passive but vigilant state, and also acted by gentle pressure of my thumbs upon such points as through the agency of the nerves were in especial sympathy with the affected parts. Water was afterwards poured upon the nape of his neck and the palms of his hands, and on the following day he came to me again much improved. On the third day he appeared at the Athenæum, before a very large and respectable audience, declaring himself quite free from pain, and able to walk without the slightest distress.

Case VII.—Pain and Swellings Cured.

ROSINA WYBELL, aged 17, servant to Mr. Chamberlain, Water Lane, Carlisle, had been afflicted nine months with a continual pain in her head and left side, accompanied occasionally by swellings of the face. She had tried medicine the whole time, under regular professional advice, but without relief. She came to me on the morning of August the 9th, 1844, weeping for pain. I threw her into the mesmeric sleep for a short time and she awoke quite well. In the evening she was mesmerised again in the presence of her master and many of the citizens. On the following day she came to thank me for the cure, saying she had never felt better in her life. When in the sleep her case presented several curious features; but there was nothing in it to me more gratifying, than the rude yet touching eloquence with which (in the dialect of the Scottish Border) she alluded, on taking leave of me, to the contrast between her sufferings before, and her enjoyment of health after the operation.

Case VIII.—Stiffness and Swelling of the Joints Removed.

Elizabeth Elwood, of Botchergate, Carlisle, had for a long time been troubled with stiffness and swelling of the ankles, which prevented her walking without the severest pain. She came to me first on the 6th of August, 1844, when I passed her into the mesmeric sleep. On being awoke she could not remember any sensations she had during her sleep, but said she was better. After being mesmerised a few more times she declared on the 10th (four days from the first operation) that she felt quite well, and was exceedingly thankful for the cure.

Case IX.—Inflammation of the Eye Cured.

Elizabeth Little, Botchergate, Carlisle, had been suffering under inflammation of the right eye, attended with severe pain in the head, for more than a year. She came to me in consequence of hearing of so many cures by mesmerism, and I passed her into the sleep, from which she awoke better. The pain was removed from the eye; a weight, she said, had been taken from her head; and her sight was clearer. A day or two afterwards, in the presence of Mr. Sheffield and other citizens she declared herself perfectly well.*

---

* I cannot proceed further in the narration of these cases, without recording my testimony to the high worth of several of the Medical Faculty in Carlisle, and the rational spirit in which they have investigated and adopted mesmerism. Indeed, the conduct of *many* of the leading men, including the late and present mayor of the city (Mr. Benwell and Mr. Steele) during my visit, made an impression upon my mind that I feel will be indelible; and whenever I think of

CASE X.—ANOTHER CURE OF TIC-DOLOUREUX.

HANNAH HETHERINGTON, Borough Street, Carlisle, had been for eight months subject to *tic-doloureux*, and had not in all that time, she said, been free from it for a single day. I mesmerised her only once, and she declared on being awoke that she felt a great change, and that she was as well as ever she had been in her life.

CASE XI.—EXTENSION OF A CONTRACTED LEG.

One of the most interesting cases I had in Carlisle was that of Mr. WILLIAM ROBINSON COWAN, of Annetwell-street, who, for many years, had been subject to a remarkable contraction of the left leg with rigidity of the knee, consequent on a severe attack of neuralgia, the original symptoms of which had been removed by strichnyne. He was unable from weakness to press his left foot to the ground, wore a high-heeled boot, used a stick, and yet halted in walking. Being mesmerised by me one evening in presence of a most numerous and respectable audience at the Athenæum, I subjected his leg to a series of manipulations by which it became extended, apparently without the slightest sensation; when, under the influence of music, he danced as freely, and almost as gracefully as I had ever seen any one. On being awoke he declared himself oblivious of all that had been done during the operation; but said that his leg now felt so flexible that he could use it with perfect freedom; and that the only inconvenience remaining was the high heel to his boot, which had to be removed. He had also now recovered so much power that he could stamp with the affected foot nearly as heavily as with the other, and could

the many cures by mesmerism there have been in that neighbourhood, it is almost impossible to avoid referring them, in some measure, to the good sense and good faith in which, by all classes, the question has been received and examined.

walk just as well without his stick as with it. Three weeks afterwards I saw him and learnt that there had been no indication whatever of a relapse, but that he could then walk with great ease and comfort.

Cases XII. to XV.—Cure and Relief of Deafness.

The power which mesmerism sometimes gives us over the senses of others is very great, and, as before contended, must have an adequate use. It enables us, when a patient has been made sufficiently susceptible, to suspend them all, either simultaneously or *seriatim*, as we please, and to restore them in the same order. It therefore follows, that where they are suspended or deranged by illness, and the patient can be brought into this requisite state of susceptibility, the operator may restore them in the same way as if they had been suspended by his own manipulations, providing there be no organic mutilation or decay. Thus, for instance, it is that in my experiments I sometimes take away the sight, and the same of smell, taste, touch, and hearing, and afterwards restore or even quicken them. Thus, too, it is that not only can any of these be suspended, but the derangement of them may be so modified that the same things shall have the most contradictory tastes, scents, or colours. And it will therefore follow, when any of these conditions occur naturally or accidentally, that they may be rectified by the same artificial process as that which would be required had they been induced by any sign or act of the operator's will. It is on this supposition only that I am at present able to offer any philosophical explanation of the following results:

ELIZABETH NICHOLSON, aged seventeen, residing with her mother, in Water-lane, Carlisle, was known to the Rev. Mr. White, of that city. She came to me during my sojourn there, exceedingly deaf. For four years she had not heard thunder, and had abstained from attendance at any place of worship because she could not hear the services. In the course of a few minutes, I threw her by the ordinary method of passes over the head and eyes into the sleep, and she awoke very much improved in her hearing. Next day I mesmerised her once in private, and again, in the evening, before a la e audience at the Athenæum, Mr. White, the minister just mentioned, being chairman, and (after she was awoke) testing her hearing in a variety of experiments, by which it was proved that she could now distinctly hear and reply to a very minute whisper made at some distance behind her. I mesmerised her again on the fourth day from our first interview, when she considered herself quite cured, and able to hear as well as she could wish.

MARGARET WALSH, daughter of Mrs. Maria Walsh, Castle-street, Carlisle, had been partially deaf from the age of two to that of fifteen years. I only mesmerised her in public, and after a few operations she declared herself quite well.

One or two other cases of deafness I shall allude to, not that they were cured, but because of the interesting phenomena they presented:—

The first is that of a fine, intelligent young gentleman, aged nineteen, of a highly respectable family in Nottinghamshire. He was *totally* deaf and mute from infancy, not being able to hear a gun fired at a few paces distance. By placing my thumbs and his in juxta-position, and looking him intently in the face, I one day threw him into a deep mesmeric trance; but however deaf he might be when awake, he could hear distinctly enough when mesmerised; since, on the introduction of a musical box, he beat accurate time to its tunes with his fingers, and seemed highly pleased with his newly-found power. Upon this we had him removed to a room in which there was a pianoforte, to the notes of which he danced and waved his body in the most correct time possible; and finding his way at last to the instrument, took hold of and embraced it with very delight. He also drew several sketches better than he could have done in so short a time had he been awake. Whilst he was standing, I touched his head in the region of *Veneration*, when he slowly bowed his knees and raised his hands. Then I touched his eyelids with a view to excite *Language*, upon which he repeated the Lord's Prayer with his fingers in the signs by which the dumb are accustomed to converse. This was to me a most touching sight, especially as his parents and sisters were all standing by with tears—but not tears of sorrow—streaming down their cheeks. What, however, struck us as most curious in this case was, that when I endeavoured to excite his organ of *Tune*, he went immediately to the piano and began to strike the keys as though he would have played over again the air to which he had just been dancing. When awoke he did not believe the sketches he had drawn were his own; and when informed of all he had done he was still more sceptical, until convinced by his father's very solemn assurance of the facts. I have yet a hope that this young gentleman may be made to hear as well when awake as when in the trance.

The other case is that of a young woman, RACHEL MONKS (living at 33, Trinity-buildings, Carlisle), who had been *totally* deaf nearly seventeen years. I mesmerised her on the 9th of August, 1844, and in the course of that day she heard the whistle of a locomotive engine at the distance of a furlong, and also heard her sister calling to her in a moderately loud voice. At night I mesmerised her again, and afterwards she heard a violin played at some distance behind her. Next morning she heard every knock at the door of my lodgings, although she sat in a room thirteen yards distant from it, and seemed highly delighted. Being compelled to leave the city immediately afterwards, I gave instructions to her friends to continue the process, but am not at present aware with what result. The fact that the sense could be appealed to in any degree in cases apparently so hopeless, is very important to the humane inquirer.

CASES XVI. AND XVII.—STAMMERING, &c.

When stammering is the result of imitation or sympathy, nothing is more easy than to remove it by the same law. The same may be said of the abnormal action or inaction of any organ, or class of organs, not accompanied by an absolute loss of vital power. As we can make others yawn with us by sympathy, so we may, in many cases, make them walk and talk like us, until the mode is established in them by force of habit. It is owing to the operation of this principle that boys playing with, or young children being nursed by, those who stammer or squint, frequently " catch" and retain the same habit—the only difference between this result and mesmerism being, that in one case the effects are produced without, as in the other they may be produced with, a specific intention. Finding in my experiments that when people had once become susceptible to me, I could in proportion to that susceptibility regulate in them the action of those vital forces which in ordinary operate as an agency between the will and the muscles, so as to cause and remove all such derangements as bear the name of St. Vitus's dance, spasmodic contortion, paralysis, agitans, strabismus, staggering or tottering in the gait, stammering, &c., it struck me that the *use* of this power would be to correct those derangements where they had occurred by nature or accident. For it follows as a matter of course, that if you can make a man imitate you in stammering, it is just as easy to make him imitate you in talking properly, until in one case as in the other the habit becomes settled. Of this, in the course of my public lectures, I have had opportunities of giving some hundreds of illustrations ; and it is often accomplished without inducing sleep or any tendency to it, by merely taking

the patient's hand, looking him in the face, and inducing him to repeat whatever words I may utter ;
after this to repeat the same or other words with me
simultaneously, and then at length let him proceed by
himself. In some cases this will have to be repeated,
perhaps frequently; but cases have not been rare in
which the cure was almost instantaneous, and if no
foolish experiments were afterwards tried, I have seldom
heard of any relapse. The following case is quoted
as an example from the *Sheffield Independent*. The
paragraph refers to two courses of lectures given in that
town in October and November, 1843:—

" On account of many people not being able to get
into the Theatre on the previous Friday evening, Mr.
Hall, early this week, announced three more lectures
for the evenings of Wednesday, Thursday, and Friday.
The audiences have again been numerous and respectable. On each evening Mr. Hall exhibited specimens
of what he believed to be the causes and cures of stammering. At the close of the lecture on Friday evening
week, a youth climbed the stage from the pit, and walked
up to Mr. Hall, requested to know (but could scarcely
make himself understood from excessive stammering)
whether he could cure him. Mr. Hall told him that he
believed he could, but requested, as it was getting late,
that he would call upon him the next day. The evening of Wednesday last Mr. Hall introduced this youth
to the audience; but, previous to saying any thing about
him himself, called on Mr. Bromley, shoe-manufacturer,
Fruit Market, requesting him to say what he knew
about the case. Mr. Bromley, in reply, stated that the
young man's name was George Langstaff; that he had
worked for him about twelve months; that he had seen
and conversed with him, on an average, several times
every week; and that all the time he had been a most
inveterate stammerer, so much so that it was difficult
for him to make himself understood, and painful for
others to listen to him. Mr. Bromley further stated,
that he was himself present at the previous Thursday

evening's lecture, and that, during the performance of
the experiments, he was in great doubt as to their truth:
they appeared too big for belief. However, with a view
to test the matter, he determined to try to get this
young man forward, which he was the means of doing
the night following. Mr. Bromley further said, that he
had conversed with the young man that day, and that
he appeared, and he believed was, perfectly cured.
Mr. Hall then asked the young man the following
questions, and requested him to answer him aloud so
that all the audience could hear him:—When did you
first see and know me? 'On last Friday evening.'—Did
it not require at least half a minute for you to utter the
first word in answering me a question? 'It did.'—How
long have you stammered? 'Seventeen years.'—Have
you during all those years, to your knowledge, spoken or
read one single sentence without stammering? 'Never.'
—Can you stammer now, in my presence, if you try?
He tried, and could not.—Mr. Hall then put a book
into the young man's hand, when he read a long passage without the least faltering in speech.—Mr. Hall
next requested to know of the audience whether any of
them witnessed the young man's coming upon the stage
last Friday evening, and whether he did not stammer
very bad? Several voices replied in the affirmative.—
He next requested the audience to say, whether there
had been the least appearance of stammering in the
young man that night? The answer was a general
'No.' The young man publicly and finally expressed his
thankfulness for what had been done for him.'

The force and pathos of the following letter from a
young gentleman of excellent character, with whom I
met on my late northern tour, would only be marred by
any comment I could make upon it. From the deep
interest he took in Sunday school teaching, his stammering was as serious a drawback on his own usefulness as on the happiness of his numerous friends:—

"Trinity Buildings, Carlisle,
"August 10, 1844.

" DEAR MR. HALL,

" According to your wish, I here give you a brief account of the particulars of my case. I learned to stammer before I had completed my fourth year. It was by imitating a female who stammered very much. Since that time my affliction has slowly, though constantly gathered strength—so much so that, until lately, I have been obliged to write down any thing of importance I had to communicate: this has been the case more especially when it became necessary to make a purchase. The many unsuccessful attempts I have made to speak, at length caused a severe pain across my breast, and I had nearly given up all hopes of being cured until I heard of your successful attempts to cure stammering. On being advised by a person who heard me stammer (Mr. Holbrook, whom I shall never forget,) to try what you could accomplish in my case, I did so, and the result has been (in less than a fortnight) an almost complete cure!

" I cannot write in the strain my full heart would dictate; but often whilst thinking of what has been done for me, I catch myself with tearful eyes. The simple but efficient mode of curing stammering which you have adopted, is doing its work upon me most evidently. Many and fervent are the expressions of wonder and pleasure that come from my friends on hearing me speak; and my father has been heard to say, that he understands more of what I say now in an hour or two, than he did before in ten years. The pain across my breast is completely gone: I stammer scarcely at all, and that only when *very much* flurried, and even then an instantaneous observance of the rules you gave me, enables me to meet almost any emergency. I have about me a sense of liberty to which, previous to my visiting you, I had been all my life a stranger; and it seems as though I had now *a right* to speak. A very marked improve-

ment has also taken place in my general health since
you mesmerised me.

* * * * * *

"I remain,
" Your obliged and grateful friend,
" JAMES MILLIGAN."

CASE XVIII.—" NATURAL MESMERISM."

On my way from Carlisle to Glasgow and Edinburgh, I lectured at Dumfries, where a young man of
the name of JOHN MURRAY, came to me complaining
of having been for about three years subject to " Natural Mesmerism." At first I was inclined to smile at
him, and asked him for an explanation, upon which he
informed me that whenever affected with grief or
vexation, his mind would become concentrated on the
cause of it, his eye would be fixed, and total insensibility would follow and continue for twenty, or from
that to thirty minutes, but that the application of cold
water to the forehead would restore him. On his recovery he had no remembrance of the state he had been
in, but if instead of being restored by the water he
were left to recover entirely by himself, he felt very
sore throughout the body for several days afterwards.
He was quite sure that from what he heard me say in
one of my lectures on mesmeric analogies, that the
state he went into naturally, was only what was often
represented in a mesmeric crisis, and he had some
belief that I could do him good. In the presence of
General Pitman and Mr. Biggar, of Maryholm, I
mesmerised him at the time, and again in the evening.
Next morning he came to me and said he felt stronger,
lighter, and altogether better than usual.

CASE XIX.—CURE OF GENERAL DEBILITY.

WILLIAM JOHNSTON, tailor, of Maxwelltown, Dumfries, had been very poorly for about six weeks, with general debility and prostration, accompanied by a severe pain in the right breast, so that he could not work. The first time I mesmerised him for this was on the 15th of August. After being mesmerised three times he was able to return to his work, and he told me on the 22nd of the month that he was well. There appeared to be a remarkable susceptibility to magnetic influences in nearly all the members of this patient's family. In two operations upon him and another, the sympathy between us was so quickened, and gave me so much power over them, as to enable me to verify the truth of what the *Lancet* said in sarcasm respecting " one person's mind moving another's limbs," and this while they were as wakeful as I am at the moment of writing the present record of the fact.

Case XX.—Restoration of an Impotent Arm and Hand by " Local Mesmerism."

In the autumn of 1844, I commenced in Edinburgh a series of experiments that appeared to excite considerable interest in the minds of very large and scientific audiences. In several of them was shown the power not only of making any particular limb, or joint of that limb, quite rigid and inert by magnetism, but, in turn, the very contrary—that of quickening, and of giving such an apparent preternatural force to its action, as would enable it easily to overcome twice or thrice the mechanical resistance that, without such a process, would be sufficient entirely to control it. Among the gentlemen who saw this tested in a variety of ways, was John Gray, Esq., proprietor of the *North British Advertiser;* and having satisfied himself, beyond all possibility of delusion, as to the validity of what he saw, he induced me to visit Dundee, for the purpose of trying if power could thus be imparted to the impotent arm and hand of one of his near relatives. The result was, to all her friends, as startling as it was gratifying. When I first saw her she was unable to raise a wine-glass to her mouth with the affected hand, or to use it for any purpose without the support of the other. All that I did was to place my left hand upon her shoulder, and with my right hand make passes down the arm, and to the ends of her fingers; for, in this case, I could not by my manipulations induce the slightest tendency to sleep, but, on the contrary, an exalted vigilance.* The consequence was, that after the first séance, which did not occupy more than ten or twelve minutes, she was able to use it with considerable ease; and after the second, she astonished all who were present by taking (with the affected hand alone) a large kettle from the fire, holding it over a table covered with china, and pouring the hot water into a tea-urn standing in the midst, apparently without the slightest difficulty or fear!

The young lady afterwards came to Edinburgh, that she might derive further benefit from these manipulations, and the result cannot be conveyed in any better form than that of the following certificate:—

"North British Advertiser Office,
"Edinburgh, Dec. 30, 1844.

" MY DEAR SIR,

" As you are about to leave town in a few days, I beg to hand you the enclosed, for the professional assistance rendered by you to Miss JESSIE RENNY, my wife's sister, who, although unable from childhood (her present age being seventeen) to use her right hand, has had the use of it so far restored by your aid, that in strength it is now fully equal to her left hand; and it only appears to require continued exercise to enable

---

* Yet many of those who pretend to test mesmerism, imagine that its claims can only be established by the induction of sleep and total insensibility. Let them become scholars of Nature, who will soon teach them that for the very reason why, in the general economy, we have power in one case to remove disease by sleep, we have a greater facility in another for inducing vigilance, if vigilance be more calculated for the patient's benefit.

E

her to use it in every respect as well as her left hand, which has at all times been perfectly strong and healthy.

" I remain,

" My dear Sir,

" Yours very truly,

" Spencer T. Hall, Esq.   " JOHN GRAY."

CASE XXI.—CURE OF ST. VITUS' DANCE.

In the month of November, 1844, I visited Perth, and was waited upon by Mr. John Douglas (manager at the office of the Perthshire Agricultural Company), whose daughter had for some time been suffering from *chorea*, or St. Vitus' Dance. Having mesmerised her once, and left instructions how they were further to treat the case, Mr. James Douglas, jeweller, of Perth, proceeded with it ; and on the 31st of December, the patient's father thus wrote to a relative in Edinburgh— the letter being at present in my possession :—

" Should you have an opportunity of seeing Mr. Hall, tell him that my daughter is quite recovered, and at school again. This is another proof of the curative properties of mesmerism, which Mr. H. will, no doubt, explain to you ; and while we meet with many taunts and jeers from the would-be learned who dispute it, we have the satisfaction of pointing her out to them."

CASE XXII.—RELIEF OF NEURALGIA.

Whilst in Dundee, in the first week of November, Mr. Durham, of 67, High-street, introduced to me his sister-in-law, who had three years before had one of her thumbs amputated, in consequence of some mysterious affection of the part which gave her the most excru- ciating pain. Instead, however, of finding relief from the amputation, it soon became evident that the painful influence had only been disturbed, not got rid of, as it now tortured the hand in the same way it had done the thumb. I made passes over the part, and instructed Mr. Durham to continue the process, and on the 11th of December he wrote me as follows:—

"In accordance with your directions, I have regularly twice a day attended upon Miss R——, since you left Dundee, and made passes over the arm and hand; and it gives me much pleasure to state, that she has for the last ten days enjoyed more ease than for three years previous; she having had in all that time scarcely two days together of freedom from acute pain; and now she has not had altogether half-a-day of any thing like pain since the second or third application. This is satisfactory in a high degree, and such as to encourage us in the continuance of your recommendation."

Case XXIII.—Relief of Paralysis.

"Another case has been put into my hands lately," continues Mr. Durham, "namely, a brother of Mr. John Todd, linendraper here, who has been paralytic upwards of twenty years, and who, I understand, you experimented on with success the day before you left Dundee. I have duly made the passes over the side affected during the last week, and am glad to state, with wonderful success, inasmuch as that he previously felt so weak in his right side generally, that it was with great difficulty he could walk the distance from his brother's shop to his own house in less than an hour, or from that to an hour and a half, and now he can do it in little more than *half the time.* He states that he feels better every way, and in my shop to-day, *he sprang from the ground to a height of nearly two feet,* an effort, he says, he never expected again to find himself able for. He is truly delighted, and expresses himself most gratefully for the little I do for him."

[It would be easy to select from the letters of my correspondents, throughout the country, as many similar

illustrations of the uses of mesmerism (after the simple
instructions given them during my itinerary) as would
form a thick volume.]

CASES XXIV. to XXVIII. — VARIOUS DISORDERS CURED OR RELIEVED.

(Copied from the *Tyne Mercury* of June 25th, 1844.)

" We are not going to discuss with Mr. Hall or his
opponents the question, as to whether the mind may
have only one, or as many as one hundred organs; or,
whether the sanative influence by which he performs
his mesmeric cures be moral, nervous, magnetic, or all
three; but we should, as public journalists, be ill performing our duty, were we to pass over in silence the
cures themselves, some of which, in this town and neighbourhood, are of a very striking character, and can be
well attested by numbers of credible witnesses, whose
names are in our possession. Indeed, we have not been
without ocular demonstration of Mr. Hall's sanative
power as a mesmeriser, in private as well as in public;
and we feel compelled to acknowledge that, however
startling some of his experiments may have been at the
lecture-room, those we have seen on highly respectable
parties in private are not less so.

" To enumerate a few of them. On Friday week
Mr. Hall was introdueed to a young lady, well known
as a talented vocalist, then staying in Newcastle. She
was suffering severely from a rheumatic affection of the
head and jaws. A tooth had been extracted a few days
previously, but without advantage. The pain continued
to agonise her until the mesmeric ' passes' were tried.
These, in five minutes, were successful in accomplishing
a *perfect cure*. A number of gentlemen, troubled with
pains in the head and giddiness, have been completely
relieved with facility, during his short stay here, by
Mr. Hall, who, so far from evincing any mystery on
the subject, goes about the business in a manner the
most unassuming and simple imaginable, contending

that every man who pretends to mystery or exclusiveness in it is a quack.

"A girl, fourteen years of age, daughter of Mr. Richardson, White Cottage, near the Walker Railway Station, has been afflicted with epilepsy for three years, the fits or paroxysms of which have attacked her violently from six or eight to sixteen or eighteen times a day, and produced a decided tendency to idiotcy. She had not, for more than a year, passed a day without a great number of these fits. Being mesmerised by Mr. Hall, on Monday, the 18th ult., she passed thirty-six hours without a fit. During eight days she had not more than five, and even they were of such a comparatively mild character as scarcely to deserve the name. The last we heard of her was that she had been three days without one, and more clear and intelligent in every respect than she had been for more than a year before.

"The officer at the Walker Station had severe pains across his loins, which rendered him unable to perform his duties without the most acute suffering. Mr. Hall happened to be casually informed of this a day or two ago, whilst waiting for the train, and instantly relieved him by the 'passes,' to such an extent that he was astonished by the effect, and declared that he could run or leap with ease and comfort were it necessary.

"A servant at the Northumberland Arms, North Shields, had been for a long time troubled every morning with violent headache, attended with nausea; Mr. Hall mesmerised her only once, more than a fortnight ago, and she has had no return of the complaint.*

"A few evenings since we had the pleasure of introducing Mr. Hall to a near relative of ours, who had been suffering dreadfully during the whole day, and indeed for the last six months, from a violent spasmodic affection of the side, accompanied by pain in the head. He threw the patient into a deep and calm mesmeric sleep, for about a quarter of an hour, and when restored to

* I saw this young woman again six months afterwards, and she had during the whole of that period been perfectly well.

vigilance no pain remained. The sceptical may ridicule this if they choose; but candid men will not repudiate the evidence of their own senses, because others may think it wise and philosophical to doubt."

CASE XXIX.—MUSCULAR CONTRACTION RELIEVED.

About the time the foregoing was published, I was one day sitting in conversation with the Rev. Mr. Campbell, of Newcastle, the Rev. Mr. Benson, of Chichester, and two other ministers of religion, who had called upon me for the purpose of discussing mesmerism, when a poor woman came in with nearly all the muscles of one side sadly contorted and stiff, and presenting a most pitiable sight. She was totally unable to open her hand, lift her elbow from her side, or walk without halting; had been twice in the infirmary for the complaint; once for eleven weeks, and again for eight weeks; had been four times cupped, and otherwise bled, blistered, cauterised, and drugged; and then discharged as incurable. So bad seemed her case, that at first I had no disposition to interfere with it, but at length (partly by persuasion of the gentlemen present), resolved to try the effect of a few manipulations. The result was astounding to those who were strange to such operations. In ten minutes she was deep in the sleep, and I then opened her hand and stretched her arm. In ten minutes more she was awake, and went out of the room lifting her hand to her head, and opening or closing it at pleasure; although, according to her own declaration, she had not seen the inside of it before for more than six years. Either of the two gentlemen above named, or the Rev. T. Pringle, of Newcastle, would, I feel sure, corroborate this statement, if necessary. But what was the result? A lady, who went round the neighbourhood delivering tracts, told the poor young woman's mother that mesmerism was a wicked thing; other discouragements were added; and, although she kept improving during the time of my stay, I have been told (though I do not vouch for its truth) that she was afterwards again taken in hand by doctors, and became as decrepid as ever. Unfortunately, whilst travelling, I lost that portion of my journal in which this patient's address and case are more particularly recorded; and, in consequence, I should have avoided any mention of it here, but for the high character of the gentlemen to whom I have referred, and the certainty that they can testify to all the material points.*

Case XXX. — Relief of an Impotent Limb in Public.

(From the *Atlas* of Feb. 15th, 1845.)

" On Wednesday evening Mr. Spencer T. Hall gave a lecture at Nottingham to a numerous and highly respectable audience. At the conclusion, about fifty gentlemen (amongst whom were Mr. Richard Howitt, the poet, and Mr. Ruben Bussey, the artist), remained to witness the simple mode in which Mr. Hall applies this subtle and potent influence as a curative. During the lecture the audience had been surprised by the speedy restoration of a stammerer to facility and distinctness of speech; but those who remained appeared much more interested by what now took place. The patient was a young woman of the name of Montgomery. She was attended by her father and several

---

* Let it not be supposed, that in the allusion here made to the report of the patient's relapse, or in what I have said of her previous treatment, it is my wish to excite any public dislike of the Faculty in Newcastle, or its neighbourhood. There, at Shields, and in Sunderland (as now in almost every town of the kingdom), there are *some* members of the profession to whom all credit is due for the manner in which they have recognised the claims of mesmerism. Whatever abuse—and there has been no little—may have been heaped by the profession, as a body, upon all the mesmerists from Dr. Elliotson downwards, no one is more ready than I am to bear witness to the humanity, skill, judgment, and candour of many of its members. Heaven forbid that I should ever forget the kindness of some of them to me, both before and since my connexion with this question!

friends ; but was altogether a stranger to Mr. Hall.
Her right arm had been contracted and useless for five
years, and she was totally unable when she first as-
ascended the platform to lift it from her side. Without
sleep, or the slightest attempt to induce it, Mr. Hall
laid one of his hands on her shoulder, and took her
fingers in the other for a few seconds, and afterwards
made about a dozen passes over the hitherto impotent
limb, when it recovered so much power that in little
more than five minutes from coming forward she retired
able to lift her hand above her head, and to use it in
putting on her shawl, amid the congratulations of her
friends and the delighted assembly. This young woman had some time before been in the General Hos-
pital fourteen weeks for the complaint, but without
any benefit."

Case XXXI.—Removal of Gangrenous Sores by Distant Treatment.

This case has some very curious and important features; and although at present the name of the patient
is withheld, I do not think he would have the slightest
objection to private reference being made to him regarding it. He is a young gentleman, the son of a
highly respectable civil engineer, in one of the midland
counties, and is both well educated and deeply read. During my sojourn at Edinburgh last autumn, he wrote me,
describing his case, saying that for some years he had
been covered from head to foot with the most virulent
sores. originating in some mismanagement whilst under
the influence of mercury which had never been eradi-
cated from his system, although no means that human
knowledge could suggest had been left untried, except
mesmerism, to which he was now desirous of resorting
as a forlorn hope. The reader will better understand
the condition to which he must have been reduced,
when told that he was so painfully sore as to be unable
to wear his braces or cravat, or to walk from home.

Under the circumstances it was impossible he could travel to Edinburgh; and as it was unlikely that I should return to England for some months, it was resolved that he should be influenced, if possible, at that distance—three hundred miles—on the principle that it was as likely for health to travel in a letter as disease.

I expect my statement of this case to meet with much scepticism and some derision : so be it. It is perfectly true, notwithstanding; and its facts are indicative of some benign influence in nature which is as potent as it is subtle, and will survive when the sceptic's laugh shall find no echo.

The object was to use some portable medium that would easily dissolve in water; therefore I took a pill, made up of materials so simple as well as soluble that the chemist smiled whilst he was preparing it for me.* This I held for some time between the palms of my hands, concentrating my mind—my hope—my faith upon the purpose. Then enclosing it in a letter, I gave the patient instructions to dissolve it in a jar of clean spring-water, of which he was to drink a portion every day, and to let me know the result about the time it became expended. He did so, and then wrote me, to my inexpressible delight, that most of his sores had disappeared! On my arrival in London, at the commencement of spring, the patient paid me a visit, and showed me numberless scars of the wounds that had been healed by this simple method, only two now remaining open; and his father, being in town on some parliamentary business, he (patient) made it convenient also to stay about a fortnight, during which time I mesmerised him daily, giving him the most refreshing though not unconscious sleep. During his visit he frequently walked several miles a-day, observing the various sights of the city and suburbs, and at parting with me expressed himself in the most delighted and grateful terms; but I begged of him very earnestly to regard

* There is nothing more convenient for this purpose than a pill of common gum, dipped in flour and enclosed in a small flat box.

me only as a *mere agent* in the case, since the influence
was from the Source whence flow all our other blessings, and that any better, healthier, and more earnest
man might have used it with still more ease and
benefit than I had done.

CASE XXXII.—CURE OF A GRIEVOUS DISORDER OF THE NERVES.

In the course of the passing summer (1845), a young
gentleman, Mr. Henry Etheredge, of Yeovil, Somerset,
came to town for the purpose of being mesmerised.
Some time before, he had been frightened by ill-treat-
ment on board ship, the consequence of which was a
general disorder of the nervous system, with an almost
total loss of memory. At the first séance I passed him
into a state of semi-somnolence, when one arm and
hand became very tremulous, and twitchings were observable in various parts of his body. In about twenty
minutes he awoke better. This was repeated about a
dozen times, the tremour and twitchings becoming on
each occasion more slight, until they ceased altogether,
and he felt well—having recovered his memory and
cheerfulness, and become physically stronger.

CASE XXXIII.—CURE OF TOOTHACHE.

A highly respectable gentleman, residing at Clapton,
came to me, complaining of an excruciating toothache.
He said, his wish was to be thrown into the mesmeric
sleep, that the tooth might be extracted without pain ;
for, as it was decayed to the nerve, he had no hope of
relief so long as he retained it. As I could not easily
bring on an insensible sleep, it was resolved that I should
act more specifically upon the tooth, with a view to
benumb the nerve. This was accomplished ; and notwithstanding the cold, damp weather that prevailed for
months after, he had no return whatever of the tooth-

ache, except once when he had probed it. The effect of this, however, was easily removed, and I saw him a long time after quite free from the annoyance.

CASE XXXIV.—CURE OF LAMENESS.

One evening, last spring, while I was staying with Mr. and Mrs. William Howitt, at the Elms, Clapton, Mr. Conrad Müller introduced a boy, about fourteen years of age, GEORGE FORD, son of Mr. Ford, farmer, of Brook-street, in that village. Three years previously, this youth had fallen from a cart, and so injured his groin that for a long time he had been compelled to keep his bed. Subsequently, however, he was so far recovered as to be able to get out with the aid of a stick, but still walked with a very awkward *twist* in his gait, and with his body bending forward, almost horizontally; and his surgeon declared that *he would be a cripple for life.* It was seeing him in this state, unable to join his companions in their games, that first excited the compassion of Mr. Müller, and induced him to advise the boy to be mesmerised, which after some slight demur, arising from their little knowledge of the process, his parents allowed.

I am the more particular in describing all the concomitancies of this case, because of the weight and respectability of those who have witnessed my connexion with it throughout, and of the unjust reports since set afloat by a medical man for the purpose of disparaging the victory that mesmerism obtained in it. What would a medical practitioner say, were I to go, after one of his cures, to the patient's mother, and by a Socratic method of cross-examination, in a conventional jargon she did not understand, suggest to her how the case *might* be explained on different principles, and then proclaim to the world that she had admitted it *could* be? He would probably denounce me and mesmerism in terms I shall not retort in this case, though richly merited. The case is well able to rest upon the three facts, that, before being mesmerised, the boy, according to his own assertion, could not walk more than a mile, though aided by a stick, without severe pain and exhaustion; that the doctor had said he would be a cripple for life ; and that in about a month after I first mesmerised him *he walked more than twelve miles in one day without his stick, and without pain or fatigue, and played in the evening as merrily as any of his companions!*

At the first séance, in the presence of Mr., Mrs., and Miss Howitt, Mr. Müller, and Miss Ford (the patient's sister), it took me nearly an hour to induce the sleep. This having been at length accomplished, I manipulated his hip and thigh for a short time, when he arose, still somnolent, reared his body nearly erect, and stamped with one foot almost as firmly as with the other. At the second séance, owing to several disturb-ing causes, I was unable to induce sleep at all. At the third he passed into it easily, and afterwards was so susceptible that I could at any time induce it in a few minutes by the simple act of taking him by the hand and standing at his side. In this way I continued to influence him two or three times a week for about two months. In his mesmeric sleep-walking he appeared to be endowed with almost preternatural strength, and marched to a martial air, or danced to a lively one, with great facility. When awoke he could generally remem-ber having heard the music, but did not appear to know that he had been dancing or speaking. I under-stand him now to be perfectly well. Of course there is still some awkwardness in his mode of walking, the result of a disproportion in the muscles of the hip from the so long-continued action of one leg and inaction of the other. But even this I think he will soon grow out of, as he now presses or stamps with one foot quite as powerfully as the other, and walks without his stick several miles every day, with his body nearly erect, and in perfect ease and comfort.

Such are some of my experiences in the use of mesmerism as a curative. It would be easy to quote a hundred other cases equally indicative of its powers; but the foregoing will be sufficient as examples. The removal of tooth-ache, nervous head-ache, slight spasms, dimness of sight, &c., is so usual that mesmerists now make but little account of such operations. Mr. T. Hudson, chemist, of South Shields, tells me that it is as common for people to go to his shop for the purpose of having such disorders corrected by a few mesmeric manipulations, as it was formerly for them to buy medicine for the same purpose. There are now several physicians in the country who regularly prescribe mesmerism, and recommend their favourite manipulators as well as their apothecaries ; and there are also many intelligent and healthy druggists in Lancashire and elsewhere who, I am told, unite both professions; whilst clergymen, private gentlemen, and even some of the nobility, are taking it up in a truly philanthropic spirit, and using it for the most beneficent purposes, gratuitously, among their poor neighbours.

It is true that some narrow-minded members of the Faculty are raising against mesmerism the most absurd and selfish cries, lest it should interfere with their practice. Nay, Dr. Cowan recently went so far as to say, in a public lecture, when speaking of the diseases which medicine had failed and mesmerism had succeeded in curing, that it must be of the devil; since, mankind being under a curse, " there were some diseases that it was never in the order of Providence intended we should attempt to cure!" When, however, I asked him as a physician and a philosopher, to tell the audience what those diseases were, he went into a rage and said he should not answer me. Poor fellow ! he could not. But it is not difficult to answer him, and I choose to do so, not in my own language, but in that of two of the most eminent physicians in Sheffield, on the occasion of my last course of lectures there. I quote from the report in the newspapers of the town :—

" Dr. CORDEN THOMPSON, as chairman, stated that, wonderful as these effects now appeared to us from their novelty, he had no doubt the day would come when the wonder would cease ; for he looked forward to the time when experience would make us as well acquainted with the natural laws by which these effects were produced, and the uses to which they might be applied, as we are with other natural operations."

" At the close of the last lecture Dr. G. CALVERT HOLLAND said, he could not allow them to part without performing what he considered to be a public duty. What they had seen that night was almost of too delicate a nature for a mixed audience; but he might truly say, he never attended a lecture wherein the experiments had been so beautiful and satisfactory. The phenomena were by them considered extraordinary, but the time was not far distant, when all that had been witnessed, intricate though it seemed, would be found as beautifully simple as the laws which regulate the circulation of the blood, or those of the planetary system. *There had been a darkness around the phenomena of the nervous system, which, as a medical man, he regretted, and which had prevented the Faculty from alleviating suffering to a degree commensurate with its prevalence.* He believed mesmerism would lift up the veil, and the men who had kept themselves aloof would be in a predicament similar to those who opposed Harvey's theory of the circulation of the blood."*

---

* How satisfactory it must be to Dr. Elliotson, and the few who through years of trial have stood by him, to find rising up everywhere talented advocates like these ! Such, however, must always be at length the solace of those who, in spite of persecution, venture beyond the prejudices of their order.

CHAPTER VII.

CASE OF MISS HARRIET MARTINEAU—AUTHOR'S INTERVIEW WITH
MR. T. M. GREENHOW—THEIR VISIT TO MISS MARTINEAU AT
TYNEMOUTH—CHARACTER OF THE PHENOMENA ARISING FROM
THE AUTHOR'S MANIPULATIONS—PROCESS CONTINUED BY MISS
MARTINEAU'S MAID—COMPLETION OF CURE BY THE VOLUNTARY
SERVICES OF A LADY—INFERENCES.

THE cure, by mesmerism, of internal tumours in the
case of Miss Martineau, after five years of severe suffering,
has naturally excited an interest commensurate with her
reputation; and though I have no desire to identify
myself unduly with the case, as my connexion with
it was but partial, there still are good reasons why it
should not be altogether overlooked in a work like the
present. It was by the especial request of the editor
of the *Atlas*, at a time when the public mind was
agitated by the most conflicting statements, and when
that gentleman thought my own unbiassed opinion on
the subject was needed, that I wrote him as follows:—

TO THE EDITOR OF THE " ATLAS."

" SIR,—You tell me that my opinions on the subject
of Miss Martineau's cure are expected by, and will be
interesting to, an inquiring public. But since Miss
Martineau herself, and Mr. T. M. Greenhow, the medical gentleman who *persuaded* me first to visit her,
vary so widely in their estimates of the case, I would
rather confine myself to a simple statement of such

FACTS relating to it as are familiar to my memory, and leave the formation of opinions upon them to the reader's own mind.

" It was about the beginning of last June, that in the calm of a beautiful evening, with a gentleman of the neighbourhood, I had been wandering on the beach, and contemplating the ruins of the old priory, and other interesting objects about Tynemouth ; when, as we were coming away from the castle-gate, my companion, pointing to a house we were passing, said—' That is the residence of Harriet Martineau.' Now, in this simple piece of information there was, for me, a world of interest, out of which arose much conversation and thought. I had read ' The Hour and the Man,' and other works of Miss Martineau, with too true a relish to be indifferent to any spot on which her occasional brilliant mental images might be moulded. Her recent refusal, too, of a public pension inspired me with regard for what I deemed in her a high sense of independence and equity ; and so I observed how pleasant it would be to see such a woman just then walking among the glorious and thrilling scenes we had left. ' Walking !' exclaimed my companion, ' she has not been able to take a walk for some years, being, poor lady, entirely confined to the house, and not expecting to walk out again. She is,' continued he, ' so reduced by some delicate internal complaint, as to be rendered almost incapable of receiving her friends ; and people of distinction, who have come far to see her, have sometimes gone away, in consequence, without that gratification.' ' What a pity,' said I, ' it is that she has no one about her who would advise her to try mesmerism (not being then aware how long she had believed in it). Were it not that it might be disagreeable, and seem obstrusive, I am sure I would write to some of my literary friends for an introduction to her, that I might have an opportunity of recommending it.' ' Do you think that mesmerism would be efficacious in such a case ?' asked my companion. ' Having known it successful in reducing wens and removing

king's evil,' was my reply, ' there are few abnormal
affections of the human system on which I would not
try it before despairing.' With such thoughts as these
we passed on, and during my stay at Shields (which
was about a fortnight) I never saw the house again
without a recurrence of them ; but my natural abhor-
rence of all assumption and meddling prevented me attempting to carry them into practice.

" In the third week of June, I was lecturing at Newcastle, which is about nine miles from Tynemouth ; and
one evening, Mr. Greenhow, who was then an entire
stranger to me, was appointed chairman and scrutineer
of the proceedings by a very numerous and respectable
audience. He appeared to observe what transpired
with remarkable scrupulosity, and worded his observations, at the conclusion, with evident caution ; but, as
some of the audience thought, rather favourably to myself, since he had before been understood to be opposed to
mesmerism, but did not now say any thing against it.
Shortly afterwards—it was on the morning of Saturday, the 22nd of the month—Mr. Greenhow called at
my lodgings to have a conference with me ; but did
not then tell me, nor had I at the time the remotest
idea, that he was in any way whatever connected with
Miss Martineau.

" There was, in Mr. Greenhow's manner such evident caution, not to say mystery or ambiguity, on this
occasion, as to put me on the defensive during the utterance of his very first sentence ; but I remembered
Nicodemus, and prepared my reply. The following, as
near as I can recollect, is the substance of our dia-
logue :—

" Mr. GREENHOW—' The experiments I saw you
perform the other evening, Mr. Hall, have certainly
impressed me as somewhat remarkable; but without
any further reference to them, I would like very well
to introduce you to a case—that of a lady who has
been long confined to the house—in which I think the

F

use of mesmerism, if true, might be tested with great advantage. I have private reasons for not naming the lady until you have given me your answer. But I may go so far as to observe, that if you knew her, you could not fail, from what I judge of your character, to feel highly gratified by such an opportunity of putting mesmerism to the test; and should you succeed I am sure you will not have reason to regret it whilst you live. The case is one of internal disorder. The chief object in applying mesmerism to it is the superseding of the use of opiates—that being all, I apprehend, you could do for it; and if you knew all the circumstances attending it, and are as enthusiastic as you seem in the desire to advance your cause, I am sure you would not refuse. The patient lives a few miles from the town, and if you think well we can go this afternoon. Yes, or no?'

"MY REPLY.—' Well, Mr. Greenhow, frank and open in all things myself, I do not like ambiguity in others. You talk of *tests*, as though you were still sceptical about mesmerism, to me, who not only believe but practise it, and since I have no more right to have faith in you, who are a doubter, than you have in me, who am an advocate; and since you are so indefinite, that it is impossible for me to know whom you would have me thus go to, blindfolded as it were; *you cannot object, if I consent, that we should be accompanied by some other medical gentleman, who is not opposed to mesmerism, that he might diagnosticate the case and watch the result. This would allow me to infer accurately at any given period, if there were any change in the patient's condition, how far that change might be owing to my manipulations. For, although there may be a powerful sanative influence exercised, it is possible we may have no speedy and striking external indication of it.* We must remember (I continued) that Great-rakes and Mesmer, in their cures, seldom or never induced that condition which is termed sleep; yet, from the general, but erroneous opinion, which now obtains, you might consider that condition to be the only test of mesmeric power.'

" Mr. GREENHOW (who had been eying me very steadily and keenly during this reply)—' What medical gentleman would you think of for this purpose?'

" REPLY—' Dr. ——, who has privately avowed to me his belief in mesmerism.'

" Mr. GREENHOW—' It cannot be. The delicacy and privacy of the case preclude it. The patient herself would object to the presence, or even cognizance, of another party."

" MY REPLY (emphatically)—' Then, sir, I am compelled, in justice to myself and to mesmerism, to decline the experiment. An apparent failure in such a case might not be set down to any peculiar idiosyncrasy, or to my own inability, or to any adventitious influence to which it might be justly due, but to mesmerism, which has already suffered too much from tests that were, in reality, no tests at all; and I would not like it to be said, when mesmerism, or what goes by that name, shall be universally recognised, that I was ever one of those who retarded it by indiscretion.'

" Mr. GREENHOW (with a slight indication of displeasure in his manner)—' You form a wrong estimate, Mr. Hall, of my own motives and the case altogether. It is delicacy and duty towards the patient alone that prevent me being more explicit with you. But as the negotiation seems now at an end, I must take your denial, for which I am exceedingly sorry, and bid you good morning.'

" As Mr. Greenhow moved towards the door, I begged him to remember that it was not from fear of a fair investigation, but of possible misunderstanding, that I had manifested so much wariness, and that if he knew all I had suffered from medical sceptics, he would not think hardly of me for the course I had taken ;— when suddenly turning again towards me, he said—

' Mr. Hall, my anxiety regarding this case—the fact that the patient herself is desirous of a trial—that she has suffered long—and that not only herself, but humanity, since she is a very kind and superior person, would gain much if you could relieve her—and as I am not myself without hope that your efforts might be of great service—I will, notwithstanding what has passed, ask you again, and I pledge myself as a man who highly values his character, that if you go with me, whatever be the result, nothing shall transpire at all inimical to your own feelings or reputation, or to mesmerism; whilst, whatever good is done, I am quite sure you will have the credit of, and the fullest justice will be done to mesmerism.'

" There seemed something so straightforward and manly in this, that my instantaneous reply was—' Since you say so, sir, I will not hesitate another moment, nor would I have demurred at all if you had said as much at first. At what time shall we start?'

" The time (I think one o'clock) was now arranged, but from some unavoidable cause we started an hour later. The railway to North Shields was the line we took—chatting on various topics till about half-way between Newcastle and Tynemouth—when Mr. Greenhow informed me, for the *first time*, that our patient was no other than Miss Harriet Martineau! The conversation during the remainder of the ride, of course, turned chiefly upon the nature of her case, her works, her genius, and public conduct. But, so far as I remember, Mr. Greenhow did not on that or any other occasion give me the slightest idea that a cure of Miss Martineau's disease had already commenced (as his pamphlet now states it had) two months before. Certainly, if it were so, he might not think it important that I should be informed. I merely state the fact that I have no remembrance of his having done so ; and as, on the other hand, Miss Martineau declares that he had twice after Christmas avowed himself compelled to give up all hope of affecting the disease, and since she further says that as to all *essential* points, she never was lower than immediately before making trial of mesmerism, every candid thinker will here see how advantageous to the truth it must have been to have had what I at first proposed—*a diagnosis of the case by some other professional man.*

"Let me now come to a good understanding with the reader. It must not be expected that in what follows I shall violate the sanctity of Miss Martineau's private home or habits, however it might gratify an impertinent curiosity to tell what from time to time I saw of one or the other. My very dear and intimate friends, William and Mary Howitt, can bear witness that so far was I ever from taking undue advantage of this popular case for my own advancement, that I hesitated to tell even them in a private answer, so late as autumn (when Miss Martineau had announced her partial cure to her relations in London), whether or not I had been connected with it. If Miss Martineau had never either given me direct leave, or published the case herself, however I might secretly have rejoiced in her recovery, the world would never have heard a word of it from me, nor shall I now, or at any time, touch upon any thing relating to it or her, that is not fully qualified by what she may herself choose to make public.

"Suffice it that after being ushered into the room in which every *séance* I afterwards attended took place—and which on that bright afternoon commanded a magnificent view of the bay opening into the ocean, and of the far-winding shores, overscattered with their countless objects of curious interest—I waited her appearance with no usual feelings. Instead of having obtruded mesmerism upon her, I had been invited at her wish to be its minister. Her case, from all I could understand, was a desperate one; such, in fact, appeared to be the unanimous opinion prevailing for at least twenty miles away. Her medical adviser (who I did not then know was her brother-in-law) I felt would regard what might occur in the light of a *test*. And when at length she

came slowly into the room, with the expression of one
that *would* be cheerful, if possible, in spite of suffering,
marks of which were evidently upon her, I regretted
that some previous acquaintance, however slight, had
not prepared us better for the undertaking.   This feeling, however, passed away ; and, as is generally the
case with me on such occasions, all other ideas were
speedily absorbed in the one paramount—the patient's
cure.   Having stated a few of the preliminary conditions, some of which appeared quite new to Miss Martineau (who did not seem aware that our cures are more
frequently performed without sleep than with it), I proceeded in all earnestness with my manipulations, of
which she has herself written so graphic and correct an
account, that I prefer giving it from her own letter of
November the 12th:—

   " ' Mr. Spencer T. Hall and my medical friend
came, as arranged, at my worst hour of the day, between the expiration of one opiate and the taking of
another.   By an accident the gentlemen were rather in
a hurry,*—a circumstance unfavourable to a first experiment.   But result enough was obtained to encourage a
further trial, though it was of a nature entirely unan-
ticipated by me.   I had no other idea than that I should
either drop asleep or feel nothing.   I did not drop
asleep, and I did feel something very strange.   Various passes were tried by Mr. Hall.   The first that appeared effectual, and the most so for some time after,
were passes over the head, made from behind,—passes
from the forehead to the back of the head, and a little
way down the spine.   A very short time after these
were tried, and twenty minutes from the beginning of
the *séance*, I became sensible of an extraordinary appearance, most unexpected, and wholly unlike any
thing I had ever conceived of.   Something seemed ιo
diffuse itself through the atmosphere—not like smoke,

---

* Mr. Greenhow was obliged to return at a specific time; and it
was thought desirable, being the first *séance*, that he should be present to the end of it.—S. T. H.

nor steam, nor haze—but most like a clear twilight, closing in from the windows and down from the ceiling, and in which one object after another melted away, till scarcely any thing was left visible before my wide-open eyes. First, the outlines of all objects were blurred; then a bust, standing on a pedestal in a strong light, melted quite away; then the opposite bust; then the table with its gay cover, then the floor and the ceiling, till one small picture, high up on the opposite wall, only remained visible, like a patch of phosphoric light. I feared to move my eyes, lest the singular appearance should vanish, and I cried out, ' O! deepen it! deepen it!' supposing this the precursor of the sleep. It could not be deepened, however; and when I glanced aside from the luminous point, I found that I need not fear the return of objects to their ordinary appearance. While the passes were continued, the busts reappeared, ghost-like, in the dim atmosphere, like faint shadows, except that their outlines and the parts in the highest relief, burned with the same phosphoric light. The features of one, an Isis with bent head, seemed to be illumined by a fire on the floor, though this bust has its back to the windows. Wherever I glanced all outlines were dressed in this beautiful light; and so they have been, at every *séance*, without exception, to this day, though the appearance has rather given way to drowsiness since I left off opiates entirely. This appearance continued during the remaining twenty minutes before the gentlemen were obliged to leave me. The other effects produced were, first, heat, oppression, and sickness, and, for a few hours after, disordered stomach, followed, in the course of the evening, by a feeling of lightness and relief, in which I thought I could hardly be mistaken.

"'On occasions of a perfectly new experience, however, scepticism and self-distrust are very strong. I was aware of this beforehand, and also, of course, of the common sneer—that mesmeric effects are 'all imagination.' When the singular appearances presented themselves, I thought to myself—' Now, shall I ever believe that this was all fancy? When it is gone, and when people laugh, shall I ever doubt having seen what is now as distinct to my waking eyes as the rolling waves of yonder sea, or the faces round my sofa?' I did a little doubt it in the course of the evening; I had some misgivings even so soon as that; and yet more the next morning, when it appeared like a dream. Great was the comfort, therefore, of recognising the appearances on the second afternoon. ' Now,' thought I, ' can I again doubt?' I did, more faintly; but, before a week was over, I was certain of the fidelity of my own senses in regard to this and more.'

" There is one essential difference between the practice of a mesmerist and that of an ordinary physician. The latter sees his patient, writes a prescription, and has no more trouble until the next interview. The mesmerist goes patiently and earnestly to work with his manipulations; and he sometimes finds, when he has carried them on for an hour, that it may be necessary for him to persevere for nearly an another; and if he have a benevolent heart (which no mesmerist ought to be without), he is too earnest to think of ceasing until he feels his work is properly done. Before and during the time I visited Miss Martineau at Tynemouth, there were many patients in Newcastle who required from me the kind of attention I have now described ; and it was something of this character that had exhausted and detained me a little on the day of our third interview, so that I arrived somewhat late, when she told me her waiting-maid had been successfully performing the same kind of manipulations as my own, and with a most agreeable effect. This pleased me exceedingly; for I am well aware that there is often as great a difference in the influence of various mesmerisers as there is in the waters that spring from different kinds of earth; and it struck me that, although my own influence in this case might be much more powerful, that of the maid might be the most salutary from its mildness;

and as she would always be at hand when wanted, I gave her such instructions as at the time seemed requisite, and went several times more—I think about six or seven in all—to see that they were duly carried out, and what the effects might be; after which my personal attentions to the case were brought to a close. Miss Martineau bears the following testimony to my services :—

" ' When Mr. Hall saw how congenial was the influence of this new mesmerist, he advised our going on by ourselves, which we did till the 6th of September. I owe much to Mr. Hall for his disinterested zeal and kindness. He did for me all he could; and it was much to make a beginning, and put us in the way of proceeding.'

" We must take Miss Martineau's own account of the first essay of her maid, and its effects. That it produced feelings which all but rendered a further use of opiates needless, and gave her a *good appetite for the first time for five years*, is a fact that common sense can much better comprehend than it could the generality of medical reports:—

" ' Within one minute (after the maid began) the twilight and phosphoric lights appeared; and in two or three more, a delicious sensation of ease spread through me—a cool comfort, before which all pain and distress gave way, oozing out, as it were, at the soles of my feet. During that hour, and almost the whole evening, I could no more help exclaiming with pleasure, than a person in torture crying out with pain. I became hungry, and ate with relish, for the first time these five years. There was no heat, oppression, or sickness during the *séance*, nor any disorder afterwards. During the whole evening instead of the lazy hot ease of opiates, under which pain is felt to lie in wait, I experienced something of the indescribable sensation of health, which I had quite lost and forgotten. I walked about my rooms, and was gay and talkative. Something of this relief remained till the next morning; and then there was no reaction. I was no worse than usual; and perhaps rather better. Nothing is to me more unquestionable and more striking about this influence than the absence of all reaction.'

"My departure for Scotland prevented me hearing much more of the case than was intimated, in very general terms, in a letter with which Miss Martineau favoured me at Dumfries, and in the inquiry of Mr. Howitt to which I have alluded, until the month of October. It was then that, at Edinburgh, Mr. Combe, Mr. R. Chambers, and Mrs. Crowe, informed me that Miss Martineau's cure was becoming a topic of conversation in select circles; and presently I received a gratifying assurance of it from Miss Martineau herself, dated the 10th of that month, in which she said that such amendment of her health had been made, that she had now 'no fear of a relapse'—that she could 'walk three miles with a relish'—that 'her maid had carried on the cure pretty far, when a benevolent lady came to her aid, out of pure zeal and kindness, and proceeded with it'—and that she could not 'feel sufficiently thankful for such a *resurrection*.' Shortly afterwards, in another letter, Miss Martineau informed me of the somnambulist, 'J,' of whom so much has been said; and, in allusion to her own case, spoke of the utter inadequacy of surgery to relieve it if mesmerism had failed, and stated that she had 'the day before walked nearly five miles, and that she had also been walking through Shields, the first time for five years she had been in a town!' Miss Martineau's last letter to me was dated the 4th of December, and in it she stated that she 'continued quite well, feeling *nothing* whatever of her late complaints.'

"Such, to the extent I have been concerned in it, is my own narrative of this cure, which may be useful as an impartial corollary to the accounts which have been published by Miss Martineau and Mr. Greenhow themselves. Still in how much the cure is itself indebted to mesmerism, or how far Mr. Greenhow's state-

ment, that the patient's ' condition in *December* is but
the natural sequel of progressive improvement begun in,
or antecedent to, the month of *April*,' may be consistent
with his conversation with and pledge to me at *Mid-
summer*, I must leave the reader to determine. But
my own solemn conviction is, that if Miss Martineau
had recovered under ordinary treatment, instead of
under that of mesmerism, there is not in the empire a
medical practitioner who would not have been exceedingly proud of the case (had it been exclusively in his
own hands), as well as decidedly opposed to an admission that ' the condition in December was *but* the *natural sequel* of progressive improvement begun in, or antecedent to, the month of April.'

" I am, sir,
" Yours, respectfully,
" SPENCER T. HALL."

" January 27, 1845."

CHAPTER VIII.

EXPERIMENTS UPON, OR AFFECTING THE AUTHOR—BY MR. J. RODGERS
AND MR. FOWLER—BY A LITTLE BOY—BY A SCEPTIC—BY MR.
SOMERVILLE BECKHAUS—BY H. S. THOMPSON, ESQ.—BY DR. EL-
LIOTSON—BY MR. HOLBROOK—BY MRS. HOWITT, AND OTHERS.

IT was not remarkable that, after seeing so much of
the influence of mesmerism upon others, I should be
occasionally desirous of knowing what would be its
effects upon myself. These have been as various as the
characters of those who operated. The first who tried
his hands upon me was Mr. John Rodgers—the next
was Mr. Fowler; but neither of them produced any
effect beyond that of soothing me into a very quiet but
not somnolent condition, by passes over the top of my
head and down the spine. The first time that I really
felt completely magnetised, was when I was trying to
produce the effect upon another—a little boy, eleven
years old, with blue eyes, light hair, fair complexion,
and of a temperament certainly not the most active.
This was in the office of Mr. Burton, printer (now the
Mercury office), Leicester. It was too soon after dinner,
so that all my nervous power was needed for the purposes of digestion, when this boy sat down to me in
presence of Mr. Burton and Mr. William Taylor, of
Nottingham, who happened at the time to be in Leicester. Having taken the boy's hands, I placed the
ends of my thumbs and his in juxta-position, and continued to look him steadily in the face for about twenty

minutes. Not observing the change in him I had anticipated, I asked him how he felt. His answer was,
"Very well." I then told him to rise, which he did;
but on trying to do the same, I found myself as fast
locked by the invisible influence to my chair as if I
had been nailed in it! The sensation now experienced
was one I can scarcely describe. Perhaps it would be
more proper to call it a lack of sensation—since, though
unable to rise from the chair, *I could not feel my contact
with it.* During the whole of this time I was, however, perfectly awake; but for the moment my condition was palpably contradictory of the adage of
"Where there's a will there's a way." The boy was at
length directed to relieve me, by wafting me with a
silk handkerchief; but owing to his not doing this very
effectively, my feelings for some hours afterwards were
any thing but comfortable.

In a somewhat similar manner I was once influenced
at Birmingham. It was on the evening of one of my
lectures that a young man called upon me at my inn,
and said he wished to be mesmerised. After some im-
portunity I consented to try him; but soon found that
instead of controlling him he was very powerfully
influencing me. This I told him; but he was very
inhumane as well as sceptical, saying that it was all
imagination on my part—that he had not influenced
me in the manner stated—nor would he, when I wished
him, use the simple means necessary for my restoration.
Since then I have generally been careful of committing
myself to any intercourse of the kind with sceptics—
who are for the most part a very inconsiderate race,
vulgarly imagining that they have a sort of right to
take up the time and strength of a believer, and then
to neglect if not to insult him when they have done.
Their self-love makes them believe it wise to doubt
what they are often in reality too ignorant to comprehend, and to talk of scepticism as something really sub-
stantial, having positive rights and claims on the believer,
which is altogether a fallacy. Scepticism at best is but

a mere negation, and has no rights at all beyond what are possessed by ignorance; but this is a lesson that some are very slow to learn. That evening at the lecture my feelings were very strange, and my mind so scattered, as it appeared, that it was with great difficulty I could arrange my thoughts consecutively and speak with the coherence necessary to the occasion. Feeling still uneasy upon returning to my inn, after the lecture, I sat for some time in company, very sad, without being able to take any part in the conversation which, for concurrent reasons, was almost entirely upon mesmerism. At length, fixing my attention upon a gentleman I recollected having seen a silent spectator and listener in the audience, and who was otherwise entirely strange to me, I felt every time he gave me an earnest look as though he could afford me some relief by manipulation. On asking him if he would mesmerise me, with the greatest readiness he complied; and not long after he had taken me by the thumbs and fixed his eyes upon mine I felt a very important change—but it was not towards sleep. A soft, warm, kindly glow stole along my nerves like a gentle tide; then came a deep sigh and a gush of tears; and lastly a high degree of vigilance and the most perfect relief from my previous unpleasant symptoms. It was after he had rendered me this courteous and friendly service, that I found the gentleman to be Mr. Somerville Beckhaus, who had already become well acquainted with mesmeric practice, and was therefore the better able (though I did not at the time of selecting him from the company know it) to remagnetise me with proper effect.

The next time I was mesmerised it was by H. S. Thompson, Esq., of Fairfield House, near York. The chief effect produced was that of a semblance of sleep, but consciousness remained. This was not, however, without great benefit to me, as it seemed to endue me with more than usual vital energy, which lasted for some time. On another occasion, when mesmerised by the same gentleman, a very different effect was produced. My sleep seemed to be more deep; but it was not common sleep. I still remained conscious; but every thing seemed to reach the sensorium through a medium more protracted than usual. When Captain Bentham, who was present, spoke, I could hear him distinctly, and yet the sound seemed to come from a greater distance, as through a lengthened and contracted passage. When he suggested to Mr. Thompson to call certain organs into play by touching my head, I was perfectly aware of what he said, and also, when the points in question were touched, what was anticipated by the process; but had neither motive, inclination, or power to give the slightest response either in word or action. At length on being awoke by the ordinary method of transverse passes and wafting, instead of feeling refreshed, as on the previous occasion, there were now a very unpleasant languor and a dulness of spirits remaining upon me. When I alluded to the difference, Mr. Thompson said that on the day before his first operation upon me he had been hunting and enjoying some other open-air exercise, by which, no doubt, he was himself invigorated; but that he had been up at a ball the night before the last séance, and that the laxity of my condition was quite correspondent with his own.

In May, 1843, I first came to London, for the purpose of delivering a course of lectures. On the journey up I had met with a serious accident by the railway which, followed by unusual fatigue on my arrival, rendered me very weary, faint, and somewhat sad at heart. Having been one morning introduced by Mr. Thompson and Dr. Simpson, of York, to Dr. Elliotson, I asked the latter before we parted if he would mesmerise me, to which in the frankest and kindest manner possible he at once consented. He began, as I sat, by looking upon me very intently and pointing his fingers towards the lower part of my brow. There was a slight gush of tears in about five minutes, and then throughout the whole frame a feeling of cool and delicious rest, but not sleep, although my eyes were involuntarily closed. I have no distinct recollection of the Doctor's manipulations after this, but think he made passes downwards from the forehead as low as the epigastrium, and from the shoulders to the hands; and in about twenty or twenty-five minutes from the commencement he recovered me by pressing my eyelids with his thumbs (with a slight jerk), and afterwards breathing a stream of warm air upon the back of my neck. I can never forget the renovating effect of this process upon me. Weeks of relaxation in the fresh green country could not have supplied me with a more agreeable vigour, and I was enabled to go through my subsequent duties with an unusual degree of animation and comfort.

Nothing to me is more remarkable than the effects produced, in turn, by the manipulations of those who have already been mesmerised by myself. The following facts are important, especially to those interested in what is called phreno-mesmerism.

There is an intelligent and estimable young man, William Holbrook, who is known to be in a high degree susceptible to magnetic influences. He is one of those upon whom I had the satisfaction of operating at various times before Liebig, Mr. George Combe, Professor Gregory, Mr. Robert Chambers, and other distinguished scientific and literary parties, in Edinburgh. I have always valued his case highly, because of its evident freedom from guile or simulation. Many, when mesmerised, are still sufficiently under the influence of ordinary motives to "help nature" in some degree ; and, without any real disposition to deceive, will endeavour to gratify the on-lookers with whatever may be anticipated or desired, by the super-addition of acts not strictly peculiar to the abnormal state they are in. Thus it is, that they will sometimes *guess*, and make mistakes, when unfair and often absurd questions are put to them, or suggested, under the supposition that they are clairvoyant, because they are then apt to partake of the wonder-loving, speculative spirit of their questioners. In Holbrook I never saw any tendency of this kind, but have always had the most perfect faith in his passiveness, under the circumstances, to what may be termed the strictest conditions of mesmerism. Still, often so strikingly beautiful and logical were his responses to phrenological excitement, that it was desirable, after the promulgation of so many hypotheses of phreno-mesmerism, to learn, if possible, whether in him the phenomena resulted in any degree from his acquired knowledge, or were solely owing to some intuitive if not organic principle. With this view I one day requested him to tell me what he actually knew of phrenology, and of the location of different organs. His reply was that, practically speaking, he knew next to nothing : his natural inclination had led him to study other matters so exclusively, that he had paid as little attention to phrenology as to any thing ; and he was not certain that he could define the location of more than half-a-dozen organs with accuracy. To test this, I asked him to place his finger upon any point of my own head, and tell me, if he could, the name of the region he was touching; but we had not proceeded far upon this plan, before I felt my whole frame thrilled by a most unusual sensation. In short, it soon became evident, that through this mode of contact he was exercising over me a most powerful magnetic influence, and, as the event proved, calling distinct faculties into excessive activity, although I still remained perfectly awake, and able to reason upon the species of " mania " he was inducing ! Directing him to apply his finger to the centre of the posterior region of my head, with a view to test, if possible, whether it was the seat of *Inhabitiveness,* or of *Concentrativeness*—I soon found my anticipation altogether over-ruled by the apparition of *two infants,* so palpably present to me, that I felt as though it would be possible to take hold of them. What is more curious, these were mother and daughter—*a dear sister of my own, as*

I had known her when an infant, and her daughter, then an infant. This was evidently a manifestation, neither of *Inhabitiveness* nor *Concentrativeness*, but of *Philoprogenitiveness;* and having no children of my own to engage that affection, it appears to have been occupied by such other fitting objects as stood nearest in relation to me.

The effect of this first excitement being removed, the operator next, by my own direction, placed his finger a little higher, when my native cottage appeared quite as palpably before me as though I had really been at and about to walk into it. This must have been *Inhabitiveness.*

On touching another point in the same region—instead of *one* sole spot—appeared to me, as if concentrated in one scene, *all* the remarkable places I had ever visited. Old cathedrals, castles, parks, mountains, forests—every place of note to which I had made a pilgrimage,—all seemed to be combined in one idea, mirrored in one glowing affection; and this was no faint vision: it appeared at the moment a striking reality.

Drawing his finger somewhat aside from the above point, towards the region marked on the charts as *Adhesiveness,* while he gently pressed it there, I saw and wished to shake hands with *one* friend alone; and then, on the point of contact being moved a little further in the same direction, I suddenly became aware, as it seemed, of the presence of *all* the friends I had ever known. This appears to me to be the seat of the *social* affections.

Subsequently by direction, he endeavoured to excite *Self-esteem, Benevolence,* and one or two other faculties; but by this time my state was much changed; I was beginning to be very confused both in my thoughts and feelings—possibly from the activity of so many conflicting principles—a slight sickness and headache supervened; and I have never since submitted to the same class of experiments—nor do I think it advisable on any occasion to induce phreno-mesmeric phenomena when the patient is in a state of vigilance, though in some cases it may easily be done.

From the above experiments it would appear that, as the results were in several instances very different from what I had anticipated, and as the operator had no motive for touching me anywhere but as he was directed, my own case does not furnish any evidence against phreno-mesmerism, although it would seem to qualify a view more amplified and modified than that at present taken by most phrenologists.

The next instance of the kind in my own experience is one, the particulars of which involving as they do the feelings of others, I am at present inclined to withhold from the world—though wishing them to be published when all parties personally concerned have departed this life. A case more beautiful and more significant of important psychical principles I have never heard or read of, even among the Germans. Suffice it now to say, that *to me* it *established* the possibility of one person putting himself in direct communication with another, *at any distance*, without the aid of any sensible medium;—nay more, it made quite evident to me the fact, that, no matter how far apart in body, persons may occasionally appear as being really present to each other, and thus interchange their thoughts as easily and clearly as if corporeally near and in regular conversation! I never wonder now at the Druids and sages of antiquity admitting none to a participation of their knowledge but such as, being first selected by themselves, were made afterwards to undergo a long process of initiation and a pledge of secresy. By any other course they would have lost one of the grandest secrets of their hold upon the mind of the world; and perhaps in their age it was well to be thus exclusive; but where once Christianity has been published, there is, I think, no further need of such mystery. Lest any one, however, attempt to abuse this power, let him be assured that if wrongly used there will be a reaction of it upon the evil-doer, with a punishment more awful than it is in the nature of an inexperienced mind to comprehend. I speak with authority, though I trust with modesty, as one who has been favoured to see far into these things. But let us for the present change the topic.

One evening when in Edinburgh, I was passing an hour with one of the most distinguished professors there, and his lady. The latter wished me to try if I could mesmerise her, but secretly determined to be the active instead of the passive party. Without having the slightest suspicion that such was her intent, I soon began to feel the magnetic influence stealing upon me to a degree that compelled me to desist, when the lady good-humouredly explained that seeing my usual homely and quiet aspect changed at the commencement of the operation into one of a more determined and lofty character, the thought was suggested to her that by a still stronger exercise of her own will she might possibly counter-influence me— and such was the effect. The influence, however, remained upon me so long as to become burdensome. All that night, and for several days and nights afterwards, I felt it haunting me in a manner that prevented any object having its natural appearance. This fact I mention to guard my readers from a repetition of the experiment. I am sure the benevolent and intellectual lady in question would not have attempted any thing of the kind, had she been at all aware of the consequences.

The last time any powerful magnetic effect was produced upon me was during the spring of this year, at Mr. William Howitt's. Our little circle had one evening been for some time engaged in a conversation on mesmerism; and many and deeply-interesting were the illustrations of it my friends quoted for me from their favourite German writers. In turn I told them many of my own experiences, and it was at length resolved that I should once again submit to the operation, and that Mrs. Howitt should be the manipulator. Standing behind me, as I sat very still, she began with slow passes over the top and back of my head, without contact. In about five minutes a *tide of sleepy influence* seemed to roll down to my feet and then back to my head. Then came a mild light, and the quiet and lovely vision of a landscape composed of the most picturesque mountains, with lakes sleeping at their feet, and a cerulean sky above. As the manipulations were varied the vision changed. The operator too began to observe effects more powerful than she had been prepared for; and I think it must have been about this time that, instead of the vast, calm landscape, I saw as it were all the colours of the kaleidescope before me. Sometimes they seemed to be fixed and beautifully arranged, as in a large cathedral window; then to be commingling and changing places with each other; and at last, as the operator became more anxious about the consequences, and I very desirous but incapable of giving her directions quietly to proceed, all seemed to vanish together in darkness, when I was awoke and immediately afterwards retired to my room. But my sleep that night was not common sleep; it was more like a long and varied half-waking dream; and on arising the next morning I had still most beautiful colours flickering before my eyes. This I attribute chiefly to the operation having been influenced by Mrs. Howitt's hesitancy when the trance should have been deepened by a continuance of the passes, which probably would soon have brought on a salutary crisis. But however free and daring in her own delightful region of song, she did not feel so brave in mesmerism; and such were the results of her humane fear of proceeding too far in a walk with which she was not familiar.

The foregoing instances will be sufficient in answer to the many who ask, " If a mesmeriser can be mesmerised?" Often when that question is put to me I say —" Yes, just as a wrestler may be overcome by one more powerful or skilful than himself; or even by one less so, if he will be passive enough while the other is active. It is not a fancy but a fact, that when one powerful magnetiser, Mr. A. A. Sparrow, approaches me, I can absolutely *feel* his presence; such was the effect even when I first saw and did not know him; and my own presence has a similar effect upon Mr. Mulholland, another magnetiser. I have also mesmerised, or hypnotised myself, by straining my eyes upon a fixed point. By this method I have been thrown into a semi-somnolent, dreamy state that has continued for hours; but do not recommend this experiment, as it has almost invariably been followed in my case by shivering, accompanied with the same kind of sensation that results from sleeping on a coach in the damp night-air—especially if left to recover slowly by myself; whilst, on the other hand, I have found no condition more tranquil and refreshing than that obtained by submitting entirely to the manipulations of an earnest, healthy, and intelligent friend, who has full faith in the efficacy of what he is attempting, and a determination to continue the operation cautiously but fairly beyond a crisis.

CHAPTER IX.

Supersentient Phenomena—Patient Hearing through the Operator—Simultaneous Muscular Action of Operator and Patient in separate Rooms—Community of Taste—Clairvoyance—" Mental Travelling" — Introvision — Mental Feeling, Taste, etc.

HAVING several times alluded to clairvoyance and other supersentient phenomena, it will be right, before concluding, to present a few unquestionable examples, as in no case have my opinions on these subjects been founded upon other than the most positive evidence, elicited with the utmost caution. It must not, however, be inferred, that because so few examples of this or any other class of phenomena have been introduced, that such cases are rare. On the contrary, great numbers of them have occurred under my immediate observation. It is to avoid tedium, that I shall confine myself to one or two illustrations of each class.

The name of Bon Gaultier will be familiar to most who are acquainted with our popular literature. This gentleman and his sister were members of a large party one evening, in Edinburgh, when mesmerism was the principal topic of conversation; and being desired to furnish the company with some evidence of its truth, I selected the young lady alluded to for a *sujet*, not only because she appeared to me to be somewhat susceptible, but because she was very deaf, troubled at the time with severe headache, and otherwise unwell, and I thought the operation would be of benefit to her. In about ten minutes from the commencement of my manipulations, she seemed completely isolated from the world, and said she knew none of its pains, but was in a region of perfect light, which, though it did not seem to come from the sun or any other object, was more bright than the sun. It was not, however, too much for her, but seemed to be a settled splendour, as mild as it was pure. This internal light increased as that of the lamps in the room was diminished. On being brought into communion with external influences, she heard some music which made her ecstatic, and after a few other experiments I awoke her, when the pain had entirely left her head, and she could hear much better, but had no remembrance of the state she had been in. Being one of those gentle and confiding beings who hope all things good of others, they who knew her had, in turn, full faith in her own integrity. The evidence furnished in her case had, therefore, great weight with the whole party ; and her brother did me the honour of writing a description of the evening's experiments, emphatically declaring his conviction of their genuineness and importance, to which Mr. John Gray (at whose house the *soirée* was given) joined and published his own testimony. The good which the young lady appeared to derive on this occasion, suggested a continuance of the treatment; and, during my stay, she became daily more susceptible. The most curious point in this case is the fact that, although some defect in the ears prevented a complete cure of her deafness, *she could, whenever I took hold of her hand, hear the remotest and minutest sounds perceptible to myself, by which it would appear that (for the time) my organs were the chief agents between the external world and her sensorium.* This at length became quite as observable when she was awake as when in the sleep. Mrs. John Gray afterwards magnetised her, and in proportion as the power of that lady over the patient increased, mine diminished.

Dr. Simpson, Mr. Williams, Mr. Thompson, Mr. Ford, and other members of the Magnetic Section of the Yorkshire Philosophical Society, will remember me operating upon a little boy in York, who, both in somnolence and vigilance, had become so susceptible that, notwithstanding the intervention of a brick wall, he would respond to whatever I might do with the design of influencing him. Thus, if I raised my hand, he would raise his own corresponding hand. If I knelt, he would do the same. If I moved any particular finger, there was a similar result. This was repeatedly tested during my stay in that city, to the perfect satisfaction of many strict investigators, although, during these experiments, there was no possibility of the boy knowing, through the ordinary medium of the external senses, what my movements were. On one occasion, he was rapidly ascending a lofty flight of steps, and had nearly reached the top, whilst I was standing at the foot, when, without the slightest precognisance, he was checked by a silent pass of my hand. Turning suddenly round, he said, " Dear me! I thought some one was coming behind and pulling me ;" and was again proceeding, when I repeated the check in the same manner, upon which he discovered the cause. This boy, like many others, could also taste and describe what was put into my own mouth.

Amongst the most candid and philosophical investigators of mesmerism I have met with are the Messrs. Bell and Mr. Coleman, surgeons, of Wolverhampton, and Mr. William Lowe, chemist, of the same town. It would be impossible for any party to manifest at once more scrupulosity and fairness than did these gentlemen on the various occasions I had the pleasure of experimenting with them : and I have no doubt that they will well remember the following facts :—One evening, in the autumn of 1843, a party of about twelve, of which they were members, met me at the rooms of a scientific institution of the town, for the purpose of quietly observing several of the more subtle mesmeric phenomena.*

One of the gentlemen operated upon was Mr. Jesse Moore, son of Mr. Moore, coal proprietor, of Walsall. With the utmost care, lest he should be induced to act and give his replies from any suggestion, one of the party, when he was in the mesmeric sleep, put several articles into my mouth, the taste of which he defined with remarkable facility and accuracy. After other experiments of a different kind, and with results quite as satisfactory, he was awoke, when another patient (a native of Sheffield) was passed into the sleep, and whilst all besides himself observed the strictest silence, without allowing the slightest possibility of his acting from suggestion, he described six articles consecutively held at a little distance behind his head, not by mere implication or inuendo (as I have heard some do, after a deal of apparent puzzling), but unhesitatingly, and in the most direct language—the articles being supplied by the parties present without any preconcert, and not held before or by the side of the patient at all, but, as previously said, at some distance *behind* him.

On another occasion, in Wolverhampton, the same patient had a watch handed to him, by Mr. Shaw, jun., with the view of learning whether or not he could read the inscription (a French one) inside it. He was but a working man, not much accustomed to reading, and when he awoke declared that he had heard very little of Paris, or of its sights. But it was curious to observe, after he had read the number of the watch *backwards,* how he proceeded to describe the various attractive sights of Paris, and afterwards the scenery along the route from that city to one of the Dutch ports—rapidly giving (as several travellers present declared) the most accurate description of the numerous objects to which he adverted. When he had done, the gentle-

* Mr. Lowe has since described some of the " phreno-mesmeric" experiments of that evening in an able article in the *Phrenological Journal.*

man to whom the watch belonged, and who was totally strange to him, and had sat listening in silent astonishment to his remarks, said that the patient had described as correctly as it was possible the route he had himself taken, and the objects he had seen immediately after purchasing the watch in Paris ! The only explanation of this phenomenon I can here attempt is, that Mr. Shaw himself, by handing the watch forward, had been placed *en rapport* with the patient; that at the moment this commenced he was thinking of the place where he had bought the watch; and finding the patient had correctly described that, and one or two of the occurrences associated with it, a sudden sense of the character of the phenomenon as now explained had come upon him, after which, by a regular ideal process, he carried him on to the termination of the journey : so that this was, in reality, but another illustration of that mental communion of which examples have been given before.

Another and not less beautiful example, omitted in the proper place, I shall, perhaps, be pardoned for introducing here, as it is so closely akin to our present subject. It is the case of a lady whose mind, besides being naturally of a very superior order, had been well educated. When I was first introduced to her, (which was in the presence of several of the most respectable and intelligent people of the neighbourhood where she resides,) she had been mesmerised a few times by another gentleman, but no phenomena of a very exalted character had up to that time been elicited in her case. It was not long, however, before I found her so susceptible to the most refined mental influences, that I had only to *think*, when she immediately gave expression to a corresponding thought. I imagined a strain of music, and she said it was as if she heard it; then a beautiful landscape, and she saw and described it as accurately as though a picture of it were before her eyes! When the music was changed, she described the difference; and when my ideal of the landscape changed, after the manner of a dis-

solving view, she described that too! One of the gentlemen present then wrote upon a paper (which she had
no opportunity of reading), what kind of a landscape
they wished me next to compose. It was to be a plain,
without a river. This she described. The next suggestion, made to me in writing, was that the plain
should have a river winding through it, and hills in
the background, with cattle grazing in the foreground,
and a house in a particular direction. Immediately
she defined this, and it was again suggested, in writing,
that I should introduce a plantation of pines at a particular bend of the river, when she said, " Stay awhile;
I also see some tall, dark trees by that beautiful curve
of the river!" During the whole of this time the
young lady was perfectly awake, and sat at a distance
from me of several yards. Other phenomena in this case
were still more beautiful and curious: but there are
reasons why at present they should be withheld.

In the winter of 1843-4, Dr. Willson Cryer, a very
candid and dispassionate inquirer, at Bradford, and
Mr. W. Prest, brought several striking cases to my
notice there. One was that of a poor weaver-boy
who, notwithstanding his sad deficiency of education,
would display, when in the mesmeric trance, as accurate a knowledge of the internal anatomy of the human
body, as if he had been a well-schooled physiologist.
At times his lucidity was marvellous, even to a mesmerist; and I always noticed that it was much more
exalted when occurring spontaneously than when has-
tened by our own eagerness, and was exceedingly liable
to be influenced by the minds of those about him; so
that when tested in an improper spirit, he would reflect the impropriety. On one occasion, Mr. Andrews, an eminent architect residing in the neighbourhood, was desirous that I should mesmerise a subject of this class, for the purpose of obtaining a diagnosis of a disease from which his lady had been suffering for a long period, and under which she was fast
sinking, without the Faculty being able to relieve or

even define it. We have the most incontestible grounds
of confidence that the little weaver-boy, whom I selected for this occasion, knew nothing of Mrs. Andrews
or her disease previously; nor of the interior of the
house in which she resided: it is even questionable if he
had noticed the existence of it before. It was arranged
that nothing should be said regarding her disease and
its previous treatment, so that it was impossible he
could speak by virtue of any inference drawn from
that source, but from his own direct perceptions alone;
since not a hint was given him as to the seat of pain,
either before or while in the sleep. When I had
mesmerised him by the ordinary mode of contact, he
went immediately towards Mrs. A., and described her
condition at the moment with an accuracy that astounded her; nor was her astonishment lessened when
he proceeded to tell her, as minutely as if he had kept
a regular diary of her case from the first, how her disease began; how it proceeded; how many, and what
kind of doctors she had consulted; and what advice
they gave her, with the effect of their various treatment, &c., defining, with the utmost accuracy, every
feature of the case from first to last, and what course
it was necessary for her then to pursue, to prevent an
extension of the disorder. Having done this, and
being left to himself for a few seconds, he suddenly
exclaimed that he could see all that was going on in
the kitchen—into which room he had never been—
describing the dresses of the people in it, the form
and colour of a dog lying near the fire, and various
other matters. Next he said he could see every plant
in the greenhouse, beyond the kitchen—although the
greenhouse had never been named, and Mr. Andrews
declared the boy could never have been in or seen it.*
He described the relative position of all the plants, as

* It ought also to be understood that I was myself a stranger in the
neighbourhood, had never been within half a mile of the house, or
in the least acquainted with Mr. and Mrs. Andrews until this occasion.

clearly as if he had himself been a party to their arrangement; and at last coming to one that especially pleased him, he was expatiating upon it, when Mr. A. asked him what was the character of the plant rising next to that he was so admiring, when he replied, with a smile, " Why, if you'll just grasp it in your hand, you'll know more about it than you wish, without learning o' me." "Right, my boy," said Mr. Andrews; "it is a prickly cactus." The same evening, being invited to meet a few of the most respectable residents, at a party given by Mr. Foster (a member of the Society of Friends), I took this boy with me, when he was no less strikingly accurate in his description of the cellars and chambers of the house (in which he never could have been), noting many things accidentally out of place, as well as others not usual in the places they there occupied, so minutely as to leave no doubt, in the minds of many who had hitherto remained sceptical regarding the higher phenomena of mesmerism, that he was perfectly lucid. It is quite clear to me, from what I have seen in the case of this boy and others, that not only are magnetic patients often cognisant of the forms and hues of the distant objects they describe, but of all their other properties. Thus, when on one occasion he was speaking of a bottle which he said he saw wrapped up, in a room over his head, he was asked what it contained. His reply was, " Wait while I've tasted," and having gone through the ideal process of tasting, he accurately described its contents. He said at Mr. Andrews' that he could *feel* the prickly cactus, and seemed to shrink with the fear of being in too close contact with it. On another occasion, when *ideally* rambling on the hills outside the town, during a snow, he said he felt chilled—although really in a very warm room—and his lips assumed a livid hue, that indicated the propriety of instantly changing his condition.

Nor have there been wanting, in addition to this exceeding susceptibility to terrestrial influences, occasions on which patients have declared themselves to be in communion with supernal objects and intelligences, among scenes and circumstances that they describe in language far more beautiful, appropriate, and impressive than they can command when in their normal state. But there are various reasons why I should not now dwell upon such cases, although the time may come when it will not be improper to discuss them freely. If, at present, I err at all, it must be on the side of moderation.

CHAPTER X.

Ultimate Tendencies of Mesmerism — Reasons why it is most believed in by the Meek and Open-minded—Its Practice in the Olden Times, and by various Nations at the Present Time, under other Names—Conclusion.

My first mesmeric impressions being those of curiosity and awe, what is the consequence of a lengthened and familiar experience? Do I feel every day led further into some new sphere of mystery, or does that which was once so wonderful and mysterious become simplified and clear? Does mesmeric practice tend to show humanity in a light altogether different to what was understood of it of yore, or to lead us back to those first natural principles, obvious to " the great forefathers of mankind," but which have been to us obscured because of our degeneracy? I think the latter. Man was made in the image or likeness of his Creator, and, in a minor sphere, calculated to reflect His attributes, as the dew-drop is a miniature reflector of the sun that, by the silent and subtle action of heat, calleth it into birth. Thus, as in the Mind of the Eternal lives the universe, which is in all its principles and phases ever manifest to Him; so to the mind of man, before it became corrupted and opaque through disobedience, was palpable whatever related to him in the world of which he is the delegated governor. No one can govern that which he does not comprehend; nor comprehend that which is not represented by some sympathetic principle in himself. But so clearly can all things relating to man be understood by him when in an uncorrupt state, that we find Moses declaring him capable of giving every thing in creation a name after its kind, significant of its functions and habits; which shows that primarily he must be a lucid being. Otherwise, how could the eagle in the sky, the ox in the meadow, the lion in the forest, and all the other varieties of animated nature have appeared to his intelligence, each either in its own place or, if not in its place, (what would be equally remarkable) with its internal functions and habits revealed to him in another place not common to it, and where it could not be manifesting those functions by its ordinary habits?* And it is a striking fact that, in all time, in proportion as men have been recalled to first principles, and have lived simple, innocent, abstract lives, their organic opacity has lessened. The grossness, hardness, and darkness of the senses, which Moses significantly symbolizes by coats of skins given to man to hide from him the nakedness of his own corrupt and degraded mind, of which he would otherwise be ashamed—and which becomes more dark as he de-

---

* Man could not, however, have been a true likeness of his Maker, unless he had been gifted in his own sphere with a likeness also of the FREEDOM which that Adorable Being universally enjoys. Hence his freedom at first to change and fall, and his freedom now to accept the invitation of Redeeming Love, and return—this being the true atonement, or *at-one-ment.* The inferior animals having had no such measure of freedom, have not so departed from the first law of *their* being, but still enjoy an intuitive consciousness of their true relation to all objects in which they have a natural interest. Thus it is that the pigeon, or the swallow, will find its way *directly* to its object, though distant a thousand miles or more; and the birds of this year will next year build their nests in like places, and of like materials to those of their parents—in a style as perfect too—*but without tuition.* If then (as even materialists allow) man be a microcosm, and have in his constitution all the qualities of the inferior creation, how can he (but that it is ordinarily veiled) have less of this kind of intelligence than these animals? To me there is nothing so wonderful in magnetic sympathy with remote objects, and the consciousness it gives us of their qualities, nor even in the power of some blind persons to distinguish colours, as in the higher instincts of the inferior animals.

H

parts further from innocence, giving himself up more
to sensuality—was no cloud to the mind of Solomon
when he lived before his Maker " as a little child;" for
we are told that he then comprehended every thing
"from the cedar on Lebanon to the hyssop that springeth
out of the wall," as well as " beasts and fowls and creep-
ing things and fishes;" but, when he departed from a
right and simple course, and became an idolator and
sensualist, he lost his wisdom and his power in proportion.   In later times, George Fox declared that as he
lived more in the spirit, and in obedience to the dic-
tates of Christ, who came to redeem man from the state
into which he had fallen through his disobedience and
sensuality, he was led more and more into a condition
in which the true nature of things appeared to him,
until he once thought of becoming a physician because
of the clear relation he saw in man to the natural circumstances in which he was placed ; but from this he
desisted, because it was afterwards shown to him that he
had a still more spiritual mission.   And how beautifully
noble George Herbert alludes to the same principle:—

> " Man is all symmetry,
> Full of proportions, one limb to another,
>   And to all the world besides.
>   Each part may call the farthest, brother;
> For head with foot hath private amity,
>   And both with moons and tides.
>
> " Nothing hath got so far
> But man hath caught and kept it as his prey;
>   His eyes dismount the highest star;
>   *He is in little all the sphere.*
> *Herbs gladly cure our flesh, because that they*
>   *Find their acquaintance there.*
>
> " For us, the winds do blow,
> The earth doth rest, heaven move, and fountains flow;
>   Nothing we see, but means our good,
>   As our delight, was our treasure;
> The whole is either our cupboard of food,
>   Or cabinet of pleasure.
>
> " The stars have us to bed:
> Night draws the curtain: which the sun withdraws.
>   Music and light attend our head.

All things unto our flesh are kind,
In their descent and being ; to our mind,
In their ascent and cause.

" More servants wait on man
Than he'll take notice of.   In every path,
He treads down that which doth befriend him
When sickness makes him pale and wan.
Oh ! mighty love ! Man is one world, and hath
Another to attend him."

How then is it that so many—even those making great
pretensions to spirituality and speaking in the most
bitter terms of materialists—how is it that they will
deny lucidity, or clairvoyance, when the senses are sub-
dued, (the office of the " coat of skins" for a moment
being suspended,) and persecute, as they do, others
who believe in that faculty?   Do not let it be for
an instant imagined that I wish to exalt mesmerism
above its natural and legitimate office.   But it is im ·
possible to avoid reprehending those who, pretending
to a belief in the spirituality of man, and being in a
continual war of words with the more honest and not
less dark professed infidel, condemn mesmerism on the
ground that " it proves too much."   My solemn conviction is, that no one, after a due examination of its
claims, can deny the *facts* of mesmerism, and at the
same time believe in the Bible !   That the susceptibility
of man to trance, somnambulism, and lucidity, with all
the mediate and intermediate conditions, is among the
institutes of creation, appears ever to have been believed
from the days of Moses.   Such states are referred to
hundreds, if not thousands of times in the religious and
scientifc histories of our race—often as resulting from a
special influence of the Divinity, and not less often as
coming from the ordinary operations of nature ; and so
vast and luminous is the evidence on this point, and so
accessible to all, that the only question which appears to
remain for our consideration, is simply as to the possibility
of the human will by signs or manipulations inducing the
same.   But it is the tendency of man to imbue whatever
he deals in with his own qualities at the moment; so that
TRUTH, however purely or freely it may flow from its

original fountain, can seldom reach the inquiring scholar in its own clearness and strength; but comes strained through the hypotheses, and coloured by the imaginations of his master, as does the light of heaven through the contracted and painted window of some ancient cloister. In process of time the scholar's mind is so adapted to this mould, and dyed in these hues, that when he in turn sets up for master, instead of leaving the tablet of his soul open, in the pure light of truth, to the forms of nature, that they may be fairly imprinted upon it as they pass, and so be given again in their pristine character to the world, he becomes merely the perpetuator of adulterations worse adulterated. This I take to be the reason why that which we now call mesmerism, or vital magnetism, or pathetism, though a PLAIN FACT to the children of Nature, and so readily believed in by unconventional thinkers, should be obnoxious as it is to those whose mental sight has become so limited and discoloured by a pedantic education, that they cannot appreciate the difference between an extension and a contradiction of our present knowledge, and are thus led virtually to denounce Nature as an impostor, because she exhibits more than they can explain or comprehend. Doubtless, there are many who will dissent from this view; but on what other principle can they explain how whole colleges of our learned opponents are able to tell, with so much gravity, who was Vulcan's mother, and in what spot the Founder of Rome was suckled by a wolf, whilst as ignorant of the fact that Solon and Plautus, and many other Grecians and Romans, were believers in mesmerism, as they are of the names by which to those sages it was known?

Leaving altogether the allusions of Scripture to the subject, and the records we have of it as an agent in the hands of the Egyptian and Grecian priesthood—of which much may be seen in Baron Dupotet's work entitled, "An Introduction to the Study of Animal Magnetism;" Mr. William Lang's work on "Mesmerism—its History, Phenomena, and Practice," and others, —it may be well to glance at the evidence furnished by men of old, who are quoted as authorities in our schools on almost every other subject. Solon (B.C. 550) is reported to have said, that " whilst the smallest hurts sometimes defy the art of physic, the gentle stroking of the hand may assuage the severest pain." Clearchus asserts, that a man appeared before Aristotle and his disciples at the Lyceum, where, by moving a wand slowly up and down over the body of a lad, he made it rigid and lifeless; but when, by a repetition of the process, he recalled the patient to himself, he told with wonderful accuracy all that had been said and done. Who can fail to perceive the identity of this process with that of modern mesmerism? Nor is it less characteristically alluded to by Plautus, a Roman, and a man of genius, who uses these remarkable words—not by way of asserting something new and startling, but as a fact already admitted, and furnishing material for an analogical argument—" as though," says he, " I were by my continued slow moving touch to make him as if he were asleep!" Tacitus also declares, that the Emperor Vespasian cured blindness in one person, and the withered hand of another, by manipulations very similar to those we read of as more recently employed by Mr. Greatrakes in similar cases; and the authority of such men as Solon, Plautus, and Tacitus, is not by any means to be treated with contempt.

But turning from these records of elder date, let us hear what analogical illustrations of the universality of this principle are furnished by travellers of the present time. Is " second-sight," in the Scottish Highlands, during semi-somnolence, a reality? Is it, or is it not true, that the barbers in some parts of China, where shaving the head is a somewhat long process, first throw their customers to sleep, by passes over the eyes, to obviate the tedium of that operation? Do northern voyagers speak the truth when they tell us that the Esquimeaux cultivate the power of throwing themselves to sleep at will, so that when danger appears which they cannot avert, they avoid its terrors by assuming a state of oblivity? Can the Fakeers of India hybernate for days or weeks together, like animals that become torpid in winter ; or be so influenced by self-mes-merising particular parts of the body as to sustain for years an abnormal position that it would torture any man in his normal state to maintain for as many mi-nutes? If not, why then the testimonies of some of our most credible travellers are altogether worthless!

Lately, in Forfarshire, at the house of the venerable astronomer, Dr. Dick, I met with Mr. Ducker, of Dover—a highly intelligent gentleman, who had spent some time among the aborigines of Australia ; and he told me, that on one occasion he went out among them to see what he then considered merely a piece of idle mummery, but which he is now convinced was a valuable process, analogous to, if not identical with, that of mesmerism. It was for curing a female of some internal disorder, and was performed in the gloom of night. A fire was kindled on the open plain, and most of the members of the tribe joined about it in a circle, and danced, whilst the patient was set apart at some distance, and the doctor or priest began his curative ceremony, which, under the circumstances, seemed odd and mystical enough. This consisted of his rapidly moving far away until hidden by the darkness, and then turning back to where the patient stood, and making passes over her for a short time with his hands from head to foot, following the outlines of her body during the process, precisely in the style of the French mesmerists, and then gliding away again, but returning and repeat-ing his manipulations at regular intervals, until the woman appeared as rigid as a statue. When released from this state she was understood to be cured. My friend, Richard Howitt,* when among these people, ob-tained similar information. Here, then, it would appear that Nature, who is too strict an economist to allow any thing to exist in vain, had suggested this genial pro-cess to those unlettered children of the wilds, by whom

* Author of many beautiful poems, and more recently of " Im-pressions of Australia Felix, during a Four Years' Residence," &c. London: Longman and Co.

it was thus successfully carried out; whilst the pedantry of London was not only denying the power altogether, but persecuting those who believed in it because, their eyes and minds being open, they could not but see it manifest everywhere.

But my object in the publication of this little work has not been so much to argue the general question, or to quote the evidence of other operators, as to add my own humble mite of experience to theirs, with the hope that those who come after us may collect the whole and benefit by the aggregation. Otherwise it might be of advantage to dwell on the use of mesmerism in suspending sensation during surgical operations, and the successful illustrations of its power in that walk, furnished by Mr. Topham, at Wellow; Mr. Hollings, at Leicester; Mr. Elliott and Mr. Castle, at Carlisle; Dr. Owens, at Wolverhampton, and many others. It has been my own office to apply it chiefly to cases of a different, though sometimes of a kindred character; and I am more and more desirous of using it in a simple and direct manner for the relief of disease rather than for any apparent purposes of divination or of mere amusement. It is a rich and powerful talent; and as it could not have been given to us that it might be hidden while in our possession, and at last returned unused; or, on the other hand that it might be wasted in the gratification of vain or unholy desires; perhaps there is no resolution with which it would be better to conclude than this:—NEVER TO EMPLOY MESMERISM, IN PRIVATE OR PUBLIC, FOR THE PURPOSE OF AFFECTING OTHERS BUT AS WE WOULD BE WILLING THEY SHOULD AFFECT US WERE WE IN THEIR CIRCUMSTANCES.

THE END.

C. WHITING, BEAUFORT HOUSE, STRAND.

Preparing for Publication,

(With Plates, illustrative of various Observations and Discoveries in Phreno-Mesmerism, Neurology, &c.)

MUSINGS ON MAN.

BY SPENCER T. HALL,

Author of "MESMERIC EXPERIENCES," &c.

Also, for Republication, by the same Author,

RAMBLES AND REVERIES

OF

A SHERWOOD FORESTER.

Who walking oft with Nature hand in hand,
Turned on her when she spoke a raptured eye;
And then, retiring to his inmost heart,
There pondered all her teachings o'er again.

OPINIONS OF MR. HALL'S EARLY WORKS.

" 'The Forester's Offering'—a volume of sterling good sense, pure English, and native poetry, the result of a combination of misfortunes and obstacles which would have broken many spirits and quenched more—appealing, however, not to our charity, but to our perception of excellence."—*Tyne Pilot.*

" It has a sparkling richness and graphicness of description, which rivet the attention and delight the mind. In its author we meet with the genuine poet, the faithful chronicler,—the child of nature ravished by the profusion of her bounties. The appearance of this work at the present time is a striking and flattering characteristic of the age."—*Sheffield Iris.*

" A very pleasing book, descriptive of forest scenery, and of many charming rural rambles—none the worse for being the production of a self-educated young man."—*Tait's Magazine.*

" The effusions of a healthful fancy and a kindly heart, worthy of a wide celebrity."—*Spectator.*

" Mr. Hall's sketches are well written: his ramble in merry Sherwood is worthy of Miller. The life of Robin Hood is a piece of literary justice. The poems are conceived and executed in a beautiful spirit. ' My Native Cottage' is written from and to the heart. * * We recommend Mr. Hall's book most heartily."—*Sunday Times.*

" He possesses a fine natural taste and great ability, and gives utterance to his thoughts with such truthful earnestness, that, by this one little work, he holds no inconsiderable place in the ranks of living authors."—*Sheffield Independent.*

" 'Rambles in the Country' are described with the enthusiasm of a genuine tourist. Mr. Hall is no common observer of things and men—he sees with the eye of a poet and 'philosopher—and his descriptions of scenes and characters are worthy of special attention. He has faith in the strength as well as in the beauty of goodness, and all his literary efforts are directed to the promotion of right feeling among his fellow-men. * * There is a sincerity and fervour in his communings with Nature that cannot fail to be impressive—he writes as if his heart were in his pen."—*Leeds Times.*

" His description of the sea is truly sublime. He is glorious by the ocean as in the forest."—*Derby Reporter.*

" ——One of Nature's gentlemen, springing up by the sheer force of original inspiration. We can well answer for this little work, that, unlike many costly vanities of the day, it is well worth reprinting. It is thoroughly a country book—full of the sunshine of free thoughts and pastoral existence, breathing of the heather and the honeysuckle, and fraught throughout with strong poetical emotion. * * The confession of his experiences at the end reminds us of Franklin, and has a noble and impressive moral."—*Atlas*, March 19, 1842.

For EU product safety concerns, contact us at Calle de José Abascal, 56–1°, 28003 Madrid, Spain or eugpsr@cambridge.org.